CW01024426

This is a thoroughly
stories about the per.
speaking person in so. ....ic *presents all of*
these in a humble, relatable style that makes one want to
read more.

> Bryon Anderson, Professor of Physics Emeritus,
> Kent State University, USA, co-author of
> *Seven Ideas That Shook Physics.*

I am grateful to have been guided so kindly into a space
where I could contemplate my own life stories.

> Bonnie Clarke, CEO Taylor Clarke, Scotland

With master stroke dexterity, Chris Mabey plops us down
where few writers dare, directly into life's innermost,
behind-the-curtains, spaces. Unrivaled autobiographical
style. Engrossing reading.

> Don Freeman, Pastor Vineyard Church of the Peninsula

The story is engaging and filled with word pictures, but
it is much more than a simple narrative. Chris manages
to wind an authentic silver thread around life, faith, and
truth, thereby offering a unique model of spiritual spring-
cleaning.

> Adrian Plass, author of *Still Crazy* and
> *The Shadow Doctor*

Dreaming
in **Provence**

Chris Mabey

© Chris Mabey, 2024

Published by Chris Mabey

A CIP catalogue record for this book is available from the British Library.

ISBN 978-1-3999-8527-7

Illustrations by Chris Mabey

Book layout and cover design by Clare Brayshaw

Prepared and printed by:

York Publishing Services Ltd
64 Hallfield Road
Layerthorpe
York YO31 7ZQ

Tel: 01904 431213

Website: www.yps-publishing.co.uk

CONTENTS

ABOUT THE AUTHOR

Chris is a writer, a psychologist, and emeritus professor at Middlesex University. He has served as a leader in four community churches in Milton Keynes. He and his wife April have four lovely daughters and many grandchildren who feature in this book.

April and me collecting stones for the house in France

FOREWORD

Apart from England, especially as May moves magically into June, France is a favourite destination for my wife Bridget and me. Some years ago, we bought and hugely enjoyed a small, two-century-old cottage in Normandy. Heaven will have to go some to compete with those crunchy, tasty trips.

In this beautifully written and crafted book, Chris Mabey brings back much of the flavour of those times. The story is engaging and filled with word pictures, but it is much more than a simple narrative.

Chris manages to wind an authentic silver thread around life, faith, and truth, thereby offering a unique model of spiritual spring-cleaning. Beware. He is quite merciless (thank God) in asking himself and his readers to consider afresh what heaven on earth really looks like, posing the kind of obtrusive questions that circle our minds like marbles in a cake-tin at midnight but tend to get shelved at dawn. Superficial tidying of faith is one thing. This is a subtle and sometimes dramatic exploration of the kingdom. Joining him might just be the best thing you ever did.

We did so love our little second home. Aah, well...

Adrian Plass, author of *Still Crazy* and *The Shadow Doctor* and a weekly blog: *Sounding the Shallows* (www.adrianplass.com)

A WELL-KEPT SECRET

The man opposite me was about my age, at ease in his casual suit, with tanned skin, slicked-back hair, and a neatly clipped moustache. We could hardly have come from more different backgrounds. Under normal circumstances, we would never have met. But he had a house to sell in northern Provence and I wanted to buy it.

Looking back, it's amazing how quickly I made assumptions that day. How little information I needed before joining the dots. He sounded public school, his manner was assured, and, within a few minutes, I gathered his occupation was gilt-edged. As an ex-RAF pilot, he'd leveraged his knowledge of aviation to set up a lucrative little business. He handled travel insurance for headline bands. It was his job to get them, their instruments, wardrobes, and roadies safe passage to the next gig on their world tour. Reliability was his middle name.

I suppose the setting helped soften me up. The Bloomsbury restaurant he'd chosen for lunch was classy. A background tide of conversation ebbed and flowed in this fluid space between work and pleasure: candidates being sized up for jobs, publisher contracts brokered, and business deals done. All this was less than ten minutes from Birkbeck (a College of London University), where at the time, I was teaching adult students Organisational Psychology.

In the mid-nineties, two couples we knew well did what the rest of us simply dreamed about. With Britain in the grip of frenetic self-absorption, their gaze shifted to the vineyards of France. Turning their backs on successful but stressful UK careers they went in search of a property to renovate. Something that they could convert into *chambres d'hôtes*, offering dinner, bed and breakfast for discerning souls. After several false starts working their way steadily south to sunnier climes, they came upon some semi-derelict farm buildings near a village called Manas.

The plot, in a forgotten corner of northern Provence where the river Drôme flows into the Rhone, looked unpromising. Undeterred by rotting roof beams and a cow byre knee deep in dung, they created five bespoke bedrooms and a gîte from the sprawling stone buildings. Stepping through a maze of paperwork and winning over suspicious locals, the project took 18 months of careful planning and hard labour.

With minutes to spare they were ready to welcome paying guests, who were buying into the dream, if only for a week or two. As the first visitors crunched up the stony drive guarded by cypress firs standing to attention like sharpened pencils, Celia was still hastily scattering cushions on the newly purchased sofas and placing flowers on window sills. Meanwhile, round the back, Bob was dismantling the scaffolding. Would the costly gamble come good? Would the sweat and tears be worth it?

The offer was seductive. Artfully furnished rooms with quirky *objets d'art* surrounded by views of slumbering fields. Large wooden, iron-studded gates creaked open onto what could have been a medieval courtyard where a table for 20 was laid. Following aperitives, a five-course meal was plated exquisitely, served and savoured, with always plenty more if needed. Among the menus on offer were confit duck, fennel and salmon in pastis with fresh asparagus, quail roasted on a tart of peas, and white wine gravy. All this was accompanied by local wines as hosts and guests swapped stories. Bob was fond of noting that the availability of quails dated back to Hannibal and his elephant trek over the Alps, with a coterie of fowl to keep his troops fed. In this ambiance, pre-holiday stresses quickly dropped away. Slipping into Egyptian cotton sheets around midnight, to the unnerving sound of silence and a sky unusually devoid of light pollution, the formula for a memorable holiday was underway.

We, like many others who sampled this unhurried lifestyle for a week here and there, were smitten. 'Tell us if you hear of a property coming onto the market', were our parting words to Bob and Celia, each time we headed back to the UK. For several years this was a fantasy request as we had no funds for such a purchase. That was until 2002 when we decided to sell my late mother's house in Bexhill-on-Sea. It was mid-May and we had a lump sum nestled in our bank account crying out to be spent. For the first time, this made a house in the Drôme stretchingly realistic.

'There's a place near us that's just come on the market. It would be ideal for you,' Celia's voice on the phone was urgent and upbeat, 'but you'd better get down here quick as others are sniffing around.' One set of sniffers was a couple we had met as comrade holidaymakers at Bob and Celia's. April and I felt awkward going into potential competition with them. Nevertheless, we booked a flight from Stansted for Friday. Only we missed it. Not for the first time, our travel plans were thwarted by cutting things too fine. As we sat wondering whether to wait all day for the next Ryanair plane, who should we spot in the Easyjet queue but our fellow sniffers, along with two children, buggies, and general child paraphernalia in tow. We went to say hello and gathered they were on their way to southern France too – no doubt on a similar mission to us. Feeling a frisson of furtiveness and bravado, we asked if we could hitch a ride at the other end as we'd missed our car hire. Then, like a set of dominoes, things fell into place: we were able to book the same Easyjet flight; they managed to upgrade their car to take us and all their equipment; we arrived at Bob and Celia's together; and we went to view the said property. At separate times, naturally.

The house, a converted tractor barn, was indeed ideal. Slightly rustic with scope for upgrading for paying guests and big enough for family gatherings. I was even beginning to compose the advertisement: '*Rural without being remote, this luxury barn with stunning views of the Ardeche....*' But perhaps I was getting ahead of myself.

A month later, I was in a Bloomsbury restaurant with the owner. Let's call him Mr Jones. He'd spent the first part of the meal enthusing about the romantic history of the house and the region. Then, over the main course, he leaned forward and said, in hushed tones:

'There are several interested parties. A French couple. But they are being picky and I'm not interested in

The offer was seductive. Artfully furnished rooms with quirky objets d'art surrounded by views of slumbering fields ... In this ambiance, pre-holiday stresses quickly dropped away.

haggling. Then there's an English couple, but they want some kind of part ownership deal, and that won't work.' He sketched their profile, and I recognised them to be our fellow sniffers. I excused myself to visit the loo. As I looked in the mirror, I frowned, splashed my face, and told myself I really must be more forthright. Was he willing to sell to us or not? On my return, my curiosity was swiftly satisfied without me having to kick his shin. Matter-of-factly, Mr Jones finally came to the point:

'This is the price. If that suits you, the house is yours.' For once in my life, for such a huge purchase, I was able to say 'yes'. We stood to shake hands like gentlemen do, and the deal was done. Or so I thought.

'Feel free to go down in July and have a good look.' He pattered on. 'My wife will be in the house and can show you around. You could even stay, there's plenty of room.'

Trying to remain as calm and dignified as an academic should, I skipped back to Birkbeck. Only falling off a log could be easier, April and I agreed when I shared the news later. In the oven heat of late July, we duly arrived at the property, with expectations bulging like our luggage.

Mrs. Jones was indeed in residence, surrounded by antique furniture and the pleasing curves of a grey mirror *armoire,* and the frothy folds of silk curtains. She was sitting on a *chaise longue* with a prim lady friend at her side. This companion turned out to be her minder. Their lemon looks told us they were not at all happy to see us and the reason soon became clear. The Jones' were divorcing. She had no intention of letting her prized French home go.

'Never mind what my husband has said. No sale has been agreed.'

For all the *Provençale* warmth, and the fact that a local *notaire* had begun drafting a contract, we felt the tumbling stones of dashed hopes. It turned out our vendors were reasonably wealthy but desperately bored with each other. Mr Jones had mentioned that their leafy Surrey home was approached by a mile-long drive. The trouble with big houses, I mused, is that it was easy to lose each other. Negotiations proceeded in fits and starts. We found ourselves to be go-betweens as their marriage disintegrated.

'Can you tell Patricia I've left a note for her on the mantlepiece in the drawing room.'

'Would it not be better if....'

'No time now, I have a flight to catch'.

We were simply wanting to acquire their French property, but here we were, obliged to pass messages from one party to the other. Mr Jones, it transpired, had 'personal vested interests' in New York and he became increasingly slippery. When I attempted to put our misgivings to him as politely as possible, I received an acid email back:

'You're the psychologist. Work it out.'

For a few days, we decamped to Bob and Celia's. The assembled holiday guests were intrigued by our attempts to buy a French property and it was a welcome diversion for everyone. Each evening, over the homemade *foie gras* or barbequed *pintarde* with their little legs in the air like upended ballerinas, they pressed us for the next instalment. Vicarious purchasers I suppose. At the end of a tortuous week of solicitor interchange, I jumped out of the shower for an urgent call from Mr Jones:

'I'm downstairs in the Court of Justice here in London. The ruling on our financial settlement includes the French house. It's being finalised this morning. I need to know that you agree to a higher price before I go back upstairs.'

This was the charming man who had misled us, lied to us, used us, and generally acted in a weasel-like manner. Now he was threatening to pull out of the deal altogether. Among the sunflower fields and ripening vines of high summer, it had all started so well.

The September sun cast deep furrows of shadow, like a vow of silence across the courtyard with its vast table, quiet now in the early morning. Chairs strewn akimbo. The ragged Russian vine linked hands with a cascading lime, and clouds of clematis were like a curtain half drawn across the stone sundial. Early fallen leaves toasted and frail, scuttled across the bleached gravel like the receding tide. Perverse imposter feelings bothered me as we tried to buy a tiny piece of this beguiling foreign land. Was our dream no more than a foolish fantasy?

As misgivings crowded in, it reminded me of another foreign land or kingdom. Sometimes cryptic and often puzzling, *kingdom* was a favourite term used by Jesus in the Christian scriptures. He used it to give his followers a taste of heaven on earth, a flavour of supernatural living. On one occasion Jesus referred to the kingdom of God first as yeast mixed into dough and then as treasure discovered in a field (Matt 13: 33; 44). Initially, these pictures are baffling. They turn so many secular norms about kings and kingdoms on their heads. A place not defended by armies and patrolled by border guards, but a spiritual space scaffolded by prayer and guarded by angels. Not so much physical territory as a state of being. Like yeast, this kingdom is barely visible and could be easily overlooked but turns out to have an enormous influence. Taking this on board, maybe I needed to relax a little regarding my French dream. After all, kneaded into the bread of everyday life, yeast exerts its quiet influence: it warms the soul, it softens the spirit, and the sweet-smelling aroma draws in those around. This kingdom is not one taken by storm but received gently.

Then there was the kingdom image of treasure. Literally, and almost accidentally, we had stumbled upon our own version of treasure in a field...a converted tractor barn, part of a disused farm in the countryside of northern Provence. In a way, it was a well-kept secret, and we dared to believe that, against the odds (obstructive owners, competitor bidders, an inflated price), it would be ours. Were we worried about losing it? Yes. Like the woman 'hiding her three measures of meal' and the man 'concealing his stash of treasure', there was a degree of cloak and dagger involved. Were we stepping out of our comfort zones? Definitely. Does God delight in being generous? Yes.

But first I need to backtrack.

2

HEAVEN ON EARTH?

It was in the penultimate year of tenure at my previous University. The late afternoon sun had finally reached my side of the building. Almost apologising for being late it now poured through the sash window of my office just as I was packing to leave. My weather-beaten leather satchel shone. It smelled as alluring as a library and was stuffed with essays to mark.

'Chris, have you got a minute?' Smiling, a colleague stood in my doorway.

It wasn't a question, it would take more than a minute and it wouldn't be funny. How good Brits are at double-talk.

He was responsible for teaching allocation. But his name badge dangling from a lanyard around his neck and the chain and bunch of keys from his belt were unnecessary. As if we were in a probation centre rather than a business school.

'I've got a train to....'

The unofficial shop steward didn't move. He was ever the informed messenger, prone to promote intrigue, I almost wanted to stop and listen. But if I missed the direct one, the slow train would lurch and stutter drearily through umpteen stops.

'The national feedback stats.' he said as if that explained all....which in a way it did, given the revenue implications for the university of being well placed on league tables. 'Our students want to see more of the professors on the undergrad programmes.'

It didn't take much to intuit what was coming.

'You've been asked to consider taking on the final year course in Leadership Development.'

In other circumstances, that could have sounded attractive. A topic I cared deeply about. Being singled out to shepherd our esteemed students to their graduation from a Russell Group university. From there they believed they would set up their own businesses, walk into plum jobs, and go places others wanted to follow. Having just, in their final year, magically been transformed into leaders. Forgive the slide into cynicism.

'We need a decision by Tuesday.' Having delivered his diktat from an unnamed source on high, my comrade-in-arms disappeared down the corridor, keys jangling. The career structure in universities comprises a very flat pyramid: lecturer, senior lecturer, professor. He was two rungs lower than me but it mattered little. He had the Pro-Vice-Chancellor team on his side. It's called referent power.

My office was an upstairs room in what was originally a women's hall of residence. It was small but boasted a chimney and tiled fireplace. No doubt in days gone by, long-skirted students would have smuggled in their tweedy boyfriends to toast muffins. The splash of sun had vanished now and the office felt drab in the gloom. For twenty years in three universities, I had relished my job: the challenge of tutoring fidgety students, the pride of being published, and the kudos of landing research grants against huge odds. Seeking, in a small way, to edge young minds from education towards enchantment...with other worlds, with alternative perspectives, with reliable reference points in a precarious post-truth world. Yet, in the space of that short interchange with my colleague, something dawned. It had been coming for a long time, but the shift towards consumerism in education still biffed me like a body blow.

I crumpled into the one threadbare, easy chair. My PC blinked at me, emotionally oblivious and of no comfort. Class photos, well-worn texts, and student gifts (Chinese fans, flimsy figurines, middle-eastern trinkets) looked down from the cramped shelves wearily. I had no objection to teaching, but I was already overloaded. I was also knee-deep in an international research project (worth a cool half million to the University). And in the margins, I chased points. In academia getting published in a handful of peer-reviewed journals had been reduced to accumulating stars. Enough stars and I became a valuable player to my university in the next national audit. Oh, and I line-managed 15 colleagues. Herding cats? Now as a cat myself I had no option but to be herded.

That day turned out to be a kind of pivot point. As the train which I finally caught dawdled through the suburbs, I reflected on the career journey I'd taken. Chasing qualifications, collecting credits, running in the fast lane, and seeking to prove myself. Yes, some skills gained and lessons learned along the way, some setbacks overcome and prizes won. Some books and papers published, some not. But when all the achievements were stripped away, what did it all amount to, I asked my shadow image in the flickering window. Even outside work, in sports, in community and church projects there was a tendency for me to seek results, to gravitate toward leading, to people pleasing. And somehow, I'd always been in a hurry.

It confirmed a choice I'd begun to make a few years back about what really mattered and what really didn't. It had started with imagining a different future. And a big chunk of that alternative scenario – although I didn't fathom its full significance at the time – was something quite unexpected. The dream of spending extended family seasons in France. Was it just a coincidence that this became a timely and welcome antidote to the breathless pursuit of reputation and rewards? My wife, April, with her Burmese mindset, was already well aware of my need to relax and be less 'driven'. It just took me a while to tumble to this truth. Maybe heaven *could* come on earth.

'Thy kingdom come, thy will be done on earth as it is in heaven.' How often I have mouthed these familiar words of the Lord's prayer (from Matthew 6:10) without registering their full impact? A heartfelt prayer that the downward spiral of unbelief and cynicism in the world be reversed? A desperate plea that flawed human tyrants be stopped in their tracks. In a world of hostile power and land grabs, I want to believe that our creator God not only sees but also cares enough to intervene and establish his *kingdom*. It seems unlikely but that's what the ancient prayer states.

As I look back on our escapades in France, the mishaps and messiness of it all, as well as the golden moments, different facets of God's kingdom catch my attention like

… the dream of spending extended family seasons in France…
Maybe heaven could come on earth.

a glinting jewel. It may seem odd to make a connection between summers among the sunflower fields of Provence and deciphering the kingdom. How does a hedonistic lifestyle possibly fit with the pietistic pursuit of God? I frequently didn't get it at the time, but I began to realise that through it all, God was at work. He was lifting the curtain on more of the plot and filling in the characters of his unfolding plan. I guess this could have dawned on me anywhere, it could have been in Finchley or Philadelphia. But it turned out to be in France.

3

TINY BEGINNINGS

Thoughts of heaven on earth, images of kingdom treasure, and miracle-working yeast were receding fast as the autumn mistral began to stir. Was our deal on the French house about to unravel? Was all the excitement premature?

From being the villain in the piece, Mrs Jones had fast become the innocent. She so wanted to stay in Drôme Provence among her Avignon antiques but the split with her conniving husband made that impossible. Now, from the basement of a London court, he was pressing me for a higher price and although it risked losing the house, I felt I couldn't budge. The price had already crept up and I stuck to our limit. He hung up in a huff. Our dream purchase tilted in the balance.

It was two hours later that news came through from Mrs Jones' solicitor. The house was ours. The solicitor, who witnessed the pressure tactics of the other party, also took the unusual step of commending us, the purchasers, for our patience and goodwill.

We were still staying at Bob and Celia's with a bunch of guests who were caught up in the brinkmanship drama. Middle-class professionals, social workers, entrepreneurs, and one person we were convinced was a spy, operating under the subterfuge of being a crop consultant in South America, all daring to dally with their own escape routes to France. That evening, I reported back on clinching the deal. There, all around the dinner table, the supportive cast in this unfolding soap opera raised their glasses. We still had a few months till the final *acte de vente* but, thanks to my mother's estate, and a sequence of benign – dare I say divine – events, a summer home in northern Provence was in touching distance. And there was money left over to install a pool and convert the garage into a studio.

It was always our intention to rent out the house for paying guests in the summer season while we moved into the adjoining studio. So, the next task was to start advertising. Not wishing to lose a season's rental, we plumped for June to open. Having a pool was the big draw, so this had to feature in our publicity. The advert generated a lot of interest and our first guests booked for mid-June. Unfortunately, our builders were behind schedule and the pool was still being filled as they arrived. The house and gardens were looking great, but there was no way of speeding up a hose. We reimbursed the total cost of their holiday. It was an expensive start to our letting business and a good lesson in salesmanship. Namely, curb my optimism, build in some slack, and keep on top of the installers.

The steady stream of guests from then on were delighted with the accommodation and continue to be, twenty years on. While we were heartened to see visitors share the Provence dream with us, in the infancy of the business there was more chastening to come, associated with the pool specifically, and water more generally.

Our stone-built house is a converted tractor barn that was originally part of the farm on the opposite side of the road. Twelve metre exposed beams hold up the roof and the once-open front has long since been filled in, providing a huge cool space for dining and relaxing. I imagine the farmers, Monsieur and Madame Bernard to be typical of the region: traditional in their ways (he still uses an electric-powered rotavator which he barely controls as it pulls him along the deep, alluvial furrows), independent-minded yet patriotic (he fought in the Algerian war), hard-working and conservative (probably voting for the Le Penn party).

We also learned that the Bernards who live across the road – and their many sons – had something of a reputation in the area for cussedness, so it wasn't a complete surprise when they objected to our pool. In their minds, it was a hazard for people walking along the track behind our property, despite it being a good 20 metres from the water. At the time the French government was legislating that all private swimming pools should be fenced off with a locked gate. We weren't enamoured with the idea of guests sitting by the pool having their uninterrupted view of the distant, mauve hills of the Ardèche pixilated by wire mesh.

This was a matter for the mayor. A different specimen to the beneficent, titular, gold-chained sponsor of good works in the UK. For a start, the French version carries out their business in a dedicated building, often the most ornate and official-looking in the village. They are the conduit of all local decisions and definitely the person to invite for aperitives at the earliest opportunity.

Bob kindly came to the meeting as our interpreter, and we listened as the Bernards laid out their complaint.

In response, we agreed to fence off the perimeter of a half-acre plot of land in which the pool sat. This was something we had decided to do anyway as neighbours tended to disregard our privacy and walk across willy-nilly, their dogs leaving presents for us to clear up. We simply asked, in return, that Monsieur Barnard use his agricultural equipment to help us erect the fence, the materials for which we would purchase. It didn't seem too much to ask, but his neck reddened in indignation at the mention of any action on his part.

As tension mounted, I felt prickly hot, dying for air-con and desperate for cooperation. Having listened patiently, the mayor sat back and folded his arms. He turned to the Bernards and said: '*I think the Mabeys are being reasonable and have agreed to a fence and an alarm.*' Then turning to us he said, without drama: ' … *and you should be aware that if the life of a member of the public is lost in your pool, you will be fined 450,000 euros.*' I gulped but could see the mayor was being even-handed. The Bernards exited the office spitting feathers in a language Bob would not translate. We left stressed but unscathed, erected the perimeter fence, and set up a movement-sensitive alarm. Unsurprisingly for an open-air pool, there was a fair bit of movement on the surface. Each time an insect or bird landed, a siren worthy of three police cars wailed. Ironically, the objecting neighbours complained. We removed the battery.

It was only when another neighbour, a telephone engineer who had retired from his job in Paris, told us that the Bernards had lost a young grandson in a tragic pool accident that the source of their vitriol became apparent. We did a mental somersault. It was April's idea to mount a charm offensive. She gathered up a large bunch of wild orchids that were peppering our lawn and took them across to Madame Bernard, who was visibly moved. Relations were on the up and when Mr Bernard offered to use his tractor to remove a huge amount of brushwood from our garden, we were the ones to be chuffed. The cherry tree we gave them in gratitude brought tears to the eyes of this weather-beaten older couple. It seems they were new to receiving kindness.

A few years later, we commissioned a Portuguese team to convert our studio into a *gîte*. This way, paying guests could stay in an independent space and we need not move out of the main house each time. They worked tirelessly, bronze-backed in the stifling heat of summer, using stone from the adjacent lavender fields to dress the external walls. With casual panache, they used angle grinders – hand-held at their waists(!) – to cut the rocks to fit.

Given that the two main labourers were named (the archangel...) *Gabriel* and *Jesús*, we felt we were in good hands, especially as the latter occasionally burst into song with snatches of operetta. A tall moustachioed man with platinum hair, I felt he would be more suited to an insurance office than a dusty building site. Did I hear him sing the Major General's song from The Pirates of Penzance? The song parodies the military leader (me) who, although well-educated, knows pretty much nothing about technology (building a gite) or warfare (project management).

It is a custom in these parts to have a housewarming when the new home is completed. It's called *prend le crémaillère*, literally 'hang the rack'. This refers to the days when the stock pot hung over the open fire for

It was April's idea to mount a charm offensive. She gathered up a large bunch of wild orchids that were peppering our lawn and took them across to Madame Bernard.

the first time and visitors arrived with contributions to pop into the communal pot. Our fireplace was now an induction hob but we improvised and invitations were issued. I wondered whether anybody would turn up. Head honcho Nelson, but sadly none of his crew of Portuguese builders, joined us. Bob the architect and Celia the interior designer, who freely admits: 'I love spending other people's money', dropped by. Then, one by one, all our neighbours appeared bearing extravagant gifts. They had, of course, peered in on various occasions during the building work, but now they had the chance to nose around properly.

I felt a gratifying thrill that everyone was getting on so well, knowing that despite the address of our domain being *Quartier d'Hôpital*, local wounds ran deep. A couple of hours later, I had given up all attempts to follow the rabbit trails of heavy dialect French spoken at the speed of a startled hare. Just as I had mentally framed a sentence, the conversation had leaped on. I looked across at the equally weary April. I do believe that if we had retired to bed, none of our guests would have noticed. Having tried so hard to dip our toe into the shallows of rural French, we were now floundering in a sea of strange words and gestures.

From a low start, relations with our neighbours were reaching a high-water mark. Unfortunately, this also applied to our wastewater system. One literal by-product of a house and *gîte* full of guests is the pressure this puts on the drainage system. Sewerage to be specific. When it was just the unforgettable Jones' abiding here the system no doubt coped. But now the ancient underground plastic tanks, full of detritus and strangled by the roots of a thirsty willow, were bubbling over at will. Perhaps not an entire coincidence, the whole family was in residence at the time. As the rain lashed down, a line of bucket holders was assembled, and the overflow was manually removed. Being knee-deep in effluent was a timely way to test the mettle and motivation of sons-in-law and suitors to our daughters. They all passed manfully. A more adequate drainage system was put in place, the installers proudly claiming that should we wish, the grey water released from the reed beds was clean enough to drink. We didn't wish.

Jean de Florette is a Marcel Pagnol novel written in the early 70s and set in the hills of Provence in the early twentieth century. A city clerk, Jean de Florette arrives to inherit a farm. The tale is one of deception, betrayal, and revenge which revolves around this newcomer whose water supply is blocked by mean neighbours. Our entry into rural Provence, our early encounters with the house, and our ongoing experience with neighbours had, in the end, been far more positive. However, there was one parallel with the Pagnol story that struck a chord for me: the enduring importance of water. In our case, having a pool filled with it was helpful; protecting the public from falling in it was sensible; dipping our toes into the linguistic shallows was challenging; and baling out the knee-deep effluent variety was character-building.

Just as Jesus described his kingdom to be like a tiny mustard seed growing into the largest of garden plants (Matt 13: 31-32), we felt our labours were beginning to bear fruit as we got absorbed into local life. Like the irrigation system, so necessary for our thirsty garden in the hot summers, it was very much *goutte* à *goutte* – drop by drop.

STARTING FROM SCRATCH

4

During our extended stays in France, I gradually learned to pick up new words and phrases, to venture beyond the present tense, but also to spot contextual cues, the naughtiness of nuance. So *'non'*, I discovered, may simply be an opening gambit from which a debate ensues. If he starts with no, the Frenchman (and it invariably *is* a man) can always work his way round to a yes, while retaining his all-important dignity.

Whether in a post-office queue, at a service counter, or collecting a car from the garage, one has plenty of time to fritter. The pace of life is less frenetic in Mediterranean climes, allowing time for even the simplest interchanges between customers and staff to be complex, pantomime affairs. Voices are raised, shoulders are shrugged, arms gesticulate, and a drama unfolds as if high matters are at stake. This is generally well-mannered but intense. Almost as though medieval jousting rules are being unconsciously invoked.

Those-in-waiting look on, or fiddle with their phones, with tolerance. Unlike me, an outsider, they've seen it all before. They know their turn will come to have the undivided attention of the patron and to engage in animated conversation. Even if it's simply to purchase a postage stamp.

For a foreigner, entry into the rural French club, or subculture, can be fraught. All I wanted was a box of matches. I waited patiently in the *tabac's* customary queue perusing the postcards and silently rehearsing my key sentence: '*Bonjour monsieur...je voudrais...*'

Then my moment finally came. But unfortunately, I was about to confuse two French nouns. I took centre stage and, with what I imagined to be a Gallic flourish, I requested *des lunettes*. My precise French pronunciation was matched by a winning grin. The shopkeeper, a squat, sooty-chinned fellow, was disconcerted. The customers behind me looked up from their phones. I sensed miscommunication on my part. Cleverly avoiding the usual Englishman's tack of saying the same thing only louder, I tried a little acting. I mimed the striking of a match on a matchbox, confident that this would secure my purchase and that the pantomime, which was getting a little embarrassing, would quickly pass. But no, the passivity of fellow customers now turned to active involvement. Strange-sounding words were being lobbed speculatively into the mêlée. The shopkeeper pointed at various merchandise on his counter, and I struck my imaginary matchbox with increasing vigour. As the mini-drama unfolded, one of the words in mid-air sounded familiar. Yes, it was *allumettes* that I wanted, not *lunettes*. I had many pairs of glasses and if I needed another, I would hardly have come to a *tabac*. I'm not sure the French for a guffaw, but as I left the shop that morning there was a lot of it about.

en face du Globe restaurant
Crest 1/6/11

I waited patiently in the tabac's customary queue ...silently rehearsing my key sentence. But unfortunately, I was about to confuse two French nouns.

Then there are the mysteries of the French language. Verbs float like daintily clad nymphs, weaving through their sentences, darting in and out at will. Nouns have quite arbitrary genders. Meanwhile, *faux amis* deceive – words that sound the same as English but carry very different meanings. Asking a Frenchman for a *journal* in a *librairie*, for example, I'd find myself buying a newspaper in a bookshop. With its acutes, graves, and the occasional circumflex, French flirts with our vowels and pulls down our defences. All is inviting. Yet, it is easy to run into a linguistic wall. To my requests and questions, French people often start with an obligatory, '*It's not possible*' or '*it's too complicated*'. The first reflex of a functionary is: '*That is not my job.*'

Of course, this does make one-way messages difficult to interpret. Like those road safety signs that digitally blink at me above the French auto-route. Some are almost poetic: '*Voyager, c'est aussie s'arrêter*' [To travel well, it is also necessary to stop....one could have an accident deciphering the meaning of that one]. '*Plus vitesse, plus urgence, plus tard*' [Too much speed, too much hurry, too late....a touch of dark humour here?]. And, after Descartes, the more philosophic: '*Je bois, donc je ne suis pas*' [I drink, therefore I am not]. OK, I did make that one up, but it does sometimes feel that an Eric Cantona-type figure, alone in a garret of central traffic control, has spotted me on the radar and is teasing me with his cryptic lyrics.

Dialogue with authority figures in France is equally ritualised, but if only it were – for me at least – as painless. Failing to learn my lesson from the *tabac*, I visited the butchers. It was a repeat case of inadequate preparation, slender vocabulary and overconfidence. I was sent out to purchase some cooked meat for lunch. Despite the fullness of the shop, each customer was treated to his or her ten minutes of undivided attention. This was part of the appeal, not just purchasing the Sunday joint but also participating in a flow of good-natured banter. The proprietor had even installed a set of five fixed cinema seats at the side of the shop interior. If they had wanted their shopping checked out by a mute machine or a monosyllabic cashier, shoppers would have gone to the local *supermarché*.

At last, my turn at the *boucherie* counter finally came, and here's where, in the fixed stare of a waiting-to-be-amused audience, I forgot my rehearsed lines. Again. I even forgot the word for meat, for goodness' sake. I put it down to the rows of pig's trotters, bull's tongues and glistening tripe grinning up at me from behind the counter. Slightly queasy, I searched desperately for the word I needed. Unlike matches, it was very tricky to act out the word *cooked*, without getting into a full-on game of charades. All I could do was blurt out *cuiller*.

Although this was not the worst approximation of the word I wanted – *viande cuite* – it was not close enough for Monsieur Boucher to work out. He stood there unhelpfully dumbfounded, rubbing his moustache. His wife bustled up beside him, a touch more eager to please. At last, a brain that wasn't on display in the delicacies cabinet. After a lot more guessing and gesticulating, she reached down and pulled out a spoon from a tray of cutlery. She raised it in triumph worthy of the *entente cordiale*. Well, what could I do? I had said '*cuiller*' and she was proferring a '*cuillère*'. Having had my allotted share of attention, I took it gratefully as if a plastic spoon was the very thing I wanted. Mustering as much nonchalance as I could, I reversed out of the shop, safe in the knowledge that I'd given the crowd in the front row cinema seats more entertainment than they were accustomed to.

The whole experience left me weirdly invigorated. I had participated in a foreign foray and left without scars, although I also left without my meat. Finding a chair outside the café, I bathed in a wave of new-found cross-cultural exuberance. I exclaimed to the young lady opposite that I felt strangely *"Excité"*. She snorted and left. Only later did I discover that saying I was aroused probably wasn't the best way to start a conversation.

Despite feeling fairly confident, I was consistently floored when attempting to engage with the locals in France. A different language, unfamiliar customs, and non-verbals that were difficult to read. To fully appreciate this new culture, it was like I had to start from scratch. Little of what I brought with me counted for anything. Although only a channel-crossing away, it sometimes felt like I was entering a foreign world. I wonder if this is what Jesus meant when he declared that to fully participate in God's kingdom it is necessary to be born anew (John 3: 3). That, for all my worldly knowledge, my education and training, even my religious aspirations, I needed to burn my bridges and leave everything behind to start afresh.

I guess there are two ways to win acceptance in a new land The first is to meticulously learn the grammar, to build a vocabulary, to finesse the phraseology and only then, when all the scaffolding is in place, seek to build a conversation with the locals. A more intuitive approach is to dive in and see what happens. Our friends exemplify these tactics. Bob was more cautious, hardly going public in French for a couple of years. In contrast to the cosmopolitan fashion designer Celia, who admits she launched in, 'speaking Italian with a French accent'. Both succeeded in the long run and are fluent now although not without some gaffes along the way. Country roads in the Drôme are perilously narrow, barely allowing two cars to pass. Garages do a brisk business in wing mirror replacements. When Celia met a cement mixer coming in the other direction, she wisely reversed onto the side of the road to let the lorry pass. In doing so it scraped her vehicle. Her subsequent explanation in novice French at the desk in the insurer's office was going well until the crucial bit. Saying she had reversed onto *la verge* sounded innocent enough, not knowing this was old French slang. The staff behind the desk were unable to keep straight faces. Celia, usually so demure, was smothered in embarrassment when she found that – in her account – she had reversed onto someone's penis. Another false friend.

REFRESHING
THE SOUL

Cycling or wandering through villages in rural France is a slowing down experience. The narrow streets and medieval archways, the stone flagstones to hidden doorways, all speak of unhurried lives and timeless charm, but often appear to be deserted. Perhaps the odd duvet airing from an upstairs bedroom, or the chatter of hens in a scruffy backyard, or a bicycle with a basket leaning against the sun-baked wall where muffled strains of the radio escape from shuttered windows. All this points to signs of life but the peeling painted sign of *Alimentation Générale* where the local grocer used to be or a faded advertisement for *Gauloises* cigarettes is suggestive of a bygone era. Most of the inhabitants, it seems, are long gone.

Yet appearances deceive. At least once a year, town squares burst into life. Trestle tables and benches appear beneath cheerful bunting that dances in the warm breeze, vats of *pistou* – a tasty stew – arrive from nearby kitchens, baguettes pile high, and wine from local vineyards stands at the ready on an impromptu bar. It could be the day of a famous saint (there are many), but whatever the excuse the *fête* is attended religiously by every villager.

Unsuspecting visitors are swept up in the commotion. Neighbour disputes and family rivalries are put aside for the day as the rumble of festivities gradually grows louder and more boisterous through to the evening fireworks, singing and dancing.

One of the first we attended was a local *fête* in Manas. Little more than a main street and a labyrinth of back alleys this village has changed little in 500 years. The church clock still chimes the farmers to their fields and calls believers to mass at the next village on Sunday mornings. In recent years it has prided itself on its *botanique* credentials with a show of specimen plants and aromatic bushes along the main thoroughfare. Impressive murals from a local artist adorn the walls leading to a wonderfully tranquil chapel restored by a village benefactor.

Lysiane and her bustling team put on a generous spread for perhaps 150 people. Less they flag, she was keen to impress her cheeses upon guests as a final course. I didn't realise how endeared we had become until I found creamy camembert being stuffed into my mouth from behind followed by an equally creamy kiss. I took her jolly but incomprehensible commentary to be a good-natured sign of acceptance of us foreigners, although it did feel like being mugged by *fromage*. As stars pinpricked the inky sky, a kerfuffle by the makeshift stage signalled an obligatory accordion being uncased. The elderly band struck up chords reminiscent of a *Parisienne* café and Edith Piaf's *je ne regrette rien* anthem was refrained in a mass karaoke. The time had come to slide out before *we* had regrets. The sound of jaunty accordion-led jazz followed and faded as we weaved down the cobbled streets.

To be welcomed, as foreign interlopers, to the bosom of village life was heart-warming. To be invited into the home of a French family even more so. One French family who has proved to be a wonderful, fixed point amidst the ups and downs of life in the Drome is Claude and Catherine.

Claude, bronzed and muscular with close-cut white hair and impish blue eyes, grew up locally and took over his father's farm. I still recall standing in one of his vast hangers, ankle-deep in a thousand balls of yellow fluff. These, were two-week-old turkeys, fluttering and screeching, destined for future dinner tables, though not typically at Christmas, as in Britain. Above the din and dust, I was caught in a crossfire of emotions: the cuteness of the little chicks, the sadness of their unsought destiny, and the livelihood of a family dependent on the restless carpet at our feet. In those days our interchange in French was stilted but there was no denying Claude's infectious enthusiasm for his newly delivered brood.

Our introduction to this family was born of necessity. In the first year of renting our French house, we needed help with changeovers, a vital ingredient to the successful wowing of holidaymakers. Claude's wife, Catherine, was recommended and so began two decades of growing friendship. When she couldn't do it herself, her daughters Emmanuelle and Alicia followed in her tracks – and sometime later her cousin Annick. They were all up to the task: hoovering with gusto, beating duvets, dusting away cobwebs, mopping tiled floors till they shone, making up beds with lavender-scented sheets scattered with cuddly *bouti* quilts.

Unlike Claude, Catherine is pretty fluent in English and not bad in German, often using these languages in her work. Indulging our attempts at French conversation, her patient correcting and suggesting has been a real boon to our linguistic progress. Where else would we have gleaned that *un nuage du lait* was a cloud of milk in tea, or *le toile d'araignee* was, literally, the gossamer fabric of a spider's web, or, talking of corners, discovered that *le bon coin* was a good place for upcycling.

How could I forget fun times together when they graciously involved us in their daily lives? Meals at their farmhouse with the girls and their boyfriends, roasting enough meat to feed a platoon of soldiers at their huge, homebuilt BBQ. And the time we arrived in the Drome from the UK having battled through a violent storm with angry thunder overhead and lightning flashing like firecrackers. How safe and loved we felt when Catherine pressed us to stay for hearty stuffed pumpkin before heading to our house. They took us on hikes in the woods of the national park around Saou, a stunning plateau approached by a geological syncline and secluded by towering peaks and a peerless volcanic plug.

Then there was the remote restaurant they proposed for a memorable evening: each of the four courses featuring snails in one form or another. Chewy, crusty, curried, quiched and caramelised. They watched our faces as we did our best to be polite and persevere. Only later did they admit that even they as hardy locals, had no wish to look another *escargot* in the eye for a year at least.

Kind, welcoming, and providing a gentle induction to rural rituals, it's amazing how discouragement can be lifted when there is wisdom and a meal in the next village. We are so thankful to Catherine and Claude for accompanying us on our Drome journey.

The narrow streets and medieval archways, the stone flagstones to hidden doorways, all speak of unhurried lives and timeless charm, but often appear to be deserted.

When a church friend, Michel, asked us to come and celebrate *la Pâque* with him and his family at his hilltop home we were again honoured. Michel is an agricultural entrepreneur, transporting live chickens by night, felling and stacking timber in the quiet months, and keeping the rabbits off his precious vegetables in the spring. Like many French of his ilk, he likes nothing more than to live off the land. It's healthy, it's convenient and, what's more, it's free. Our experience had been that French families were happy to invite us Brits to *l'apéritif,* but it took a special relationship, like that with Catherine and Claude, to infiltrate their hearth and home.

As friends and his extended family gathered on Easter Sunday, smoke from the outside oven drifted across the stone courtyard, bringing the sweet aroma of roast lamb, streaked with a generous smothering of garlic. It had been slowly roasting on the spit over a wood fire since early that morning, powered by the two-speed gearbox of a Citroen 2CV to regulate the rotation. The clanging bells of sheep and goats have been heard here on the slopes in Provence for centuries. The sign of quality, we gathered, is a free-range lamb raised from a local rustic breed, until they reach the age of three to seven months. Too young some may argue, but at least their short lives had been pampered ones; suckled by their mothers, then grass-fed, grazing freely on the hills high above vineyards below.

The day before, I'd accompanied Michel and a couple of friends to a local farm. Leaning on the rail fence to observe the carefree lambs dance around was fun, and watching Michel skedaddle around the field to catch his chosen victim had us in stitches. Having made his choice, and finally caught his victim it was taken out of sight for slaughter. I felt quite chuffed to be so close to the cut and thrust of the *traiteur's* work, but as an urban driver, I was less enthusiastic about transporting the bloody carcass in my boot.

We were delighted to sit down at mid-day to sample a traditional Easter starter of cold asparagus in a vinaigrette sauce topped with eggs and chopped chives. What we did not foresee, many courses and a liberal amount of wine later, was that we would be ensconced there for most of the day. The gentle banter and story-telling, the succession of dishes and reminiscences, made for a wonderfully relaxed extended meal. I even managed an unnoticed catnap or two.

As the French conversation bubbled around me like a verbal jacuzzi, I began to wonder about the festival we were celebrating. Friends and family had gathered on Easter day looking forward to an extended meal in convivial company. Even allowing for the appetite many French people have for deep discussion and animated analysis, what I had not anticipated was a blow-by-blow account of the multi-layered origins of the festival we were celebrating. At a purely culinary level, spit-roasting a whole lamb on a barbecue was reminiscent of Maghrebi cuisine, a dish very popular in Algeria and Morocco known as *Méchoui* or Meshwi, and often the centrepiece of Muslim family gatherings. A Jewish guest had treated us to a brief commentary on the ancient festivals associated with Passover as practiced by his community. Then, our host Michel had, from his Christian perspective, pointed to Jesus being the lamb of God.

According to the Catholic take on Easter there is a ritual in France called *la chasse aux oeufs*, an ancient rule which forbids church bells to ring on Good Friday. As Michel's wife explained, the bells are said to fly to Rome to be blessed by the Pope, returning on Sunday loaded with chocolate treats for 'good' children. A rather bizarre and elaborate way to instil discipline in one's offspring, I couldn't help thinking to myself. The announcement that *les cloches sont passés* is meant to send everyone of all ages outside to see what chocolate goodies can be found, whether sugared eggs, chocolate bunnies, or flying bells, all symbolic of Easter. I wasn't sure that any of the children present, who had long since left the conversation, saw the connection between the chocolate eggs they'd consumed and the Easter resurrection of Jesus.

Tradition has it that these treats are consumed after the final course, which is usually the first strawberries of the season. Our table was hopelessly out of sequence. Any signs of chocolate were on the kids' faces rather than in the garden. The whole-day meal was drawing to a close. It was dark outside, and our magnificent hosts were finally showing signs of fatigue.

An unfailing benefit of spending time in France is the delicate, varied, and nuanced tastes of the meals served in restaurants and at the dinner tables of French hosts, the wonderful flavours of the wines that dance upon the palate chosen to complement the food. Not just this but the care taken in preparing, presenting, and serving local specialties. Our experience of inclusive fetes, our socialising with Claude and Catherine, and our Easter with Michel teach me to savour the unhurried time of such occasions with family and friends. My senses tell me that this kind of hospitality – which can be enjoyed in many countries, not just France of course – is highly desirable and speaks of kingdom values. Yet, is not God's kingdom even more than this? It points to something even more special and sustaining than pleasing my palate or filling my stomach? The hospitality God which offers shapes my life, gives it meaning, and soaks my soul with joy.[1]

---

1   Romans 14:17 The Message Bible, Eugene Peterson.

6

LIFETIME
GUARANTEE

I was in an upstairs room of Monsieur Gautier Sayagh, having been ushered in by his wife. He was leading my gaze to his latest gismo, a streamlined, transparent cylinder, with leads attached. Was I looking at a state-of-the-art aquarium? I could see no tropical fish. Was it a vacuum cleaner robot waiting for instructions? Seemed unlikely, as the room was spanking clean. No, although this was a modest villa that resembled many other private homes in the small village of Manas, I was standing in a dental surgery. Gautier lived 'below the shop' as it were.

'This is only one of five in France,' he boasted in impeccable English, 'you see these laser points at each end. Your replacement tooth will be held here in the middle, a replica peg made of fibre-reinforced porcelain, and cut from multiple angles with precision.'

'How does it know the...er... shape?' I asked, disturbed at the thought of a small, disembodied part of my mouth being sculpted and then re-inserted as an implant.

'The 3D photo we take of your molars, we feed it in. No need to send X-rays to the clinic. No waiting three weeks to get the pictures back. I can do it in 15 minutes.'

He chattered fast, clearly excited by the prospect of having a guinea pig Brit to try out his hi-tech toy. I was sure the charge for making an impression in my mouth would also make a healthy impression on his bank balance.

'Let me think about it,' I said, already convincing myself that the oral ache I came in with was receding.

To give him credit, Mr Sayagh didn't push it. It's almost as if he knew that, having explored all other options, I'd be back, begging for his state-of-the-art laser treatment.

Having procrastinated for too long, I finally sought out my dentist's surgery when we were back in the UK. Shouldered by a tanning salon on one side and Costa Coffee on the other, it had an unassuming frontage with its logo imprinted on frosted glass. It was airy and modern, not a white coat or whizzing drill in sight. All rather reassuring. Talia at the reception desk dealt with me efficiently enough, as if I were checking into a hotel. She registered my details.

'From our records, I see that your last visit was ...' she clicked the mouse, '...just over three years ago.' It felt like my teacher was handing back an especially disappointing essay. She looked up over her owl-like spectacles. 'And that was to see the hygienist'. I nodded sheepishly recalling that it was less a casual, dropping-in visit and more a full-scale assault on my molars with sharp, twangy instruments.

Tugged by a touch of guilt, I followed her to a windowless interior room for a longer set of questions posed by the dentist herself, a formidable lady called Jacky. Her name badge glinted in the artificial light.

'No, I haven't been to a dentist for several years.'

'Yes, I do brush my teeth twice daily.'

'Yes, I do floss…er… when I remember.'

'No, I do not use an electric toothbrush.'

'Yes, I do have a heart condition (which is worsening by the minute) …'

Jacky was giving away nothing as she recorded her findings. Whatever secret mission I was being recruited for, I had a sinking feeling that my credentials were falling short. Still, if my afternoon appointment consisted of completing questionnaires, I would be happy. After all, I used to devise surveys for a living.

My relief was short-lived. I suppose it was unrealistic to expect that my dental work could be replaced with a pleasant conversation with no invasion of social or oral space. Nicole was waiting for me in the next room and so began the methodical dismantling of my defences. First, to be lain prostrate on a cushioned chair, and bedecked with a bib. I resisted all temptations to be infantilised and tried a grown-up conversation.

'If you don't mind me saying, you look very young to be a dentist.' That is the best I could do from a sun-lounger position.

'I recently graduated.'

'…in?'

'in ancient history at Durham.'

'Ah…' I smothered a cough, 'and have you found a career yet?'

'Not yet. It is very pleasant here'.

'So how long have you been working for this surgery?'

'Two months,' she said brightly

I wanted to say, 'What on earth qualifies you to enter my mouth?' Not wishing to be ruder than I had already been, I came up with some lame connection between archaeology and rotting teeth. She smiled a practised smile.

It turned out that Nicole was just the warm-up act, the dental assistant. Jacky now marched back in pulling on surgical gloves. 'What appears to be the problem?'

Several answers came to mind. 'Your assistant is mis-qualified.' 'I have a pathological fear of dentists.' 'I seem to have come into the wrong shop.' As it was, since the whole room screamed 'Don't mess with these guys', I decided to be compliant. I pointed vaguely towards the back of my mouth where the pain, over recent days, had become more and more tangible. But given current circumstances, entirely tolerable.

'Ok let's take a look.' said Jacky swinging an interrogation lamp into my face, while Nicole simultaneously lowered my chair to horizontal, perhaps judging me to be a flight risk. In quick succession, Jacky yanked and probed, rattling off numbers duly charted on Nicole's clipboard.

Sitting up for a breather, I tried to sound breezy and knowledgeable: 'So lots of threes, that's good, eh?'

'We are measuring inflammation associated with periodontal disease. Three equals a pocket of 3 to 5 mm depth.'

I was going off Jacky fast.

But now came the cosy bit. An X-ray of my teeth appeared on the wall and we all three clustered around as if viewing a recent Alpine holiday. Sadly, the shadows on the north-facing side of the 'mountains' indicated where remedial work was needed. Even though my jaw already ached and I was ready to go home, we were still at base camp.

'Can I suggest we work on these four here today?' Jacky said. As if it was a question. As if I had any choice. As if it was something we were going to do together, roped at the waist on some imposing cliff-face.

Lying flat again, local anaesthetic was injected into my upper gum. Manfully I grimaced and tried not to flap my arms like Mr Bean. Nicole was playing 'good cop', and after these minor terrors asked if I'd like to rinse out my mouth. Raising me to a sitting position I gratefully took the plastic cup of pale, violet liquid. The numbing from the anaesthetic was almost instant, so my attempt to drink left me dribbling out of the side of my collapsed mouth. It got nowhere near the mini-sink to my left. Like a naughty schoolboy, I looked at the puddle on the floor. Robbed of feeling, denuded of dignity, disgraced by the erosion of my neglected teeth, I was at a low ebb.

I thought of those carefree customers next door sipping their flat whites. Oh, to be in an adult world again. Even to be turning to light toast on a sunbed just a few metres through the wall in the other direction. Anywhere was a better place than where I was...

'We're going to sort this out for you.' Jacky's definite voice broke into my daydream as if we were setting out on an expedition. I liked her confident tone but just wish the pot-holing could take place in someone else's cavities. Back to horizontal, I was once again utterly at the mercy of all the instruments that an ancient history graduate and a rugged surgeon could simultaneously probe into my mouth.

Above the clamour of machines humming, suction hissing and drills whirring, Jacky calmly announced: 'I'm going to put a 'raincoat' in there to catch any debris.'

With studied coolness, the young couple with Frappuccino smiles in Costa pretended not to see the demented man pawing at the window.

I didn't think it was raining but was in no position to resist. Nicole helpfully placed some kind of gauze shield across my throat. I risked opening my eyes and through plastic goggles noticed for the first time that there was a TV screen helpfully placed on the ceiling. Serena Williams was playing her quarter-final match and momentarily I was transported to the soporific punt and grunt of Wimbledon. Then the uniformed bosom of Jacky pressed against my face, obscuring my vision and I remembered where I was. By degrees, I had been regressing to babyhood and now the carefully choreographed process was complete.

My sight was impaired. I was supine and helpless. All I could hear was alien sounds. My tongue was gagging beneath the gauze: was this a spoon, a teat, a dummy?

Mild pain pervaded my whole body from my head down. And I needed a pee.

Again, it was Nicole who spotted my non-verbal contortions. 'Is everything OK?'

'Arghhh...I...I... naargh, warghhh.' Did she really expect me to speak? I waved toward my nappy region and pulled a pleading face.

Instruments were withdrawn, swabs were swiftly removed, and the antiseptic-white room reeled as I rose from the chair. Serena had set point. Jacky's and Nicole's voices faded as I staggered towards the door and corridor beyond. I made it to the front entrance and the sunlit precinct beyond. I gulped in the non-sterilised afternoon air. The young couple with Frappuccino smiles in Costa looked so normal. With studied coolness, they pretended not to see the demented man with a bloodied bib and dribbling mouth pawing at the window.

Talia, the receptionist, was very good at helping restore my dignity. She had intervened before I'd reached the door and directed me to the loo. Escaping the premises turns out to have been a delusion on my part. She calmed me down, gently removed the plastic goggles, and I straightened my jacket. A few minutes passed and then an invoice chattered innocently from the printer. I would gladly have paid double to bring the treatment plan to an end. But no. I was confronted with a choice: a list of pot-holing adventures with Jacky and Nicole stretching out for the months to come or succumbing to a French high-speed, laser zip-wire. The latter suddenly seemed the way forward.

It was a month later and we had returned to France. 'Ah, hello Dr Mabey, you're back with us.' Monsieur Sayagh's tone betrayed a whiff of self-satisfaction.

'Good afternoon.' I tried to smile, 'Do what you have to with that thingy of yours.'

Like remedying toothache, my life seems to be full of attempts to seek comfort, crave security, avoid pain, and promote pleasure. Natural instincts for sure, but I was learning that sometimes I needed to let go. Getting the best treatment – whether in France or the UK – entailed a step-by-step de-powering (the chair, the bib, the searchlight) rendering me docile. I wanted to be in charge, but it became obvious that yielding to the experts was the wise option. Uncomfortable though this was. Maybe there was a parallel here. I needed to yield not just to my dentists but to my Creator!

Curiously, this helped me decode another of Jesus' enigmatic instructions to *seek first his kingdom and his righteousness, and all these things shall be yours as well.'* (Matthew 6:33). Much like the dream of an untroubled, leisured lifestyle, revolving around France, as soon as I started to cling to that dream and it became the end goal, the contours of this kingdom receded and became fuzzy. It was into this very natural restlessness that God injected a stunning reality. I was realising that my inner self – my soul – would not rest until it had found its home in him. As a result, I held the dream more lightly. Counter-intuitively, as I placed him and his priorities foremost, I found clarity and fulfilment returning. All the mundane things I chased after somehow fell into place.

7

POWER NOT TALK

Identical silver statuettes adorn our bookcase in France. The figure of a tennis player making a backhand groundstroke. I wish I could say they were solid silver and that the dates weren't just stuck on – somewhat underwhelmingly – to each respective base. I am pretty proud of this mini trawl of trophies. Doubles Champion of the *Charols All-Comers Tennis Tournament* sounds quite impressive. Not just once but three times. Perhaps the foundation for this small achievement was laid back in my youth.

There is something special about being up before everyone else, especially in the summer. Even if it's going to be a hot day, at 5 a.m. there's a freshness in the air and a sense that the world is yours, untainted by the chatter of voices, the whoosh of traffic. As a teenager, this was my all-time favourite holiday job. I had my own float as a milkman at the local dairy. Once on my round, I was as chirpy as a chaffinch in an apple tree.

It was the heady summer of '67. While paisley-patterned hippies were floating to San Francisco with flowers in their hair to Scott Mackenzie's soundtrack, I did my share of milk-floating. The job happened to coincide with the Wimbledon Schoolboys national tennis tournament. In a wild moment of fantasy, our PE teacher at school, Mr Baker, had entered Stephen Masters and me as a doubles team.

When I explained to Reg, the dairy manager, that I couldn't do my milk round on Monday because I was playing tennis at Wimbledon, he did a little skip of excitement. 'Don't worry,' he said, 'I'll take over your round for the morning,'

Well, we duly lost the first match. But rather than being the end of our participation, it meant we were entered into the plate competition for first-round losers. And after that, we suddenly became invincible. Each day, Mr Baker drove us up to southwest London and each day we won, qualifying for the next day's match. Reg was a lot less chipper by Friday but still seemed to feel my success reflected well on his modest village dairy.

I played field hockey for my university and dribbled at soccer, earning the nickname 'twinkle-toes'. But my main game was tennis.

And so, to a late surf of fame. In my fifties, I made an innocent choice: to enter *Le Tennis Tournoi*. The small village of Charols in Drôme Provence boasts a shop, a bar, several boules' courts, and an unusually well-maintained, tarmac tennis court with flood lights. Pinned to the notice board there was an invitation to enter the annual tournament. Having paid my five euros entrance fee, the next day I saw from the *inscription* that I had been paired up with Sylvain. I imagined this to be a young East European, a non-podgy female prodigy. But my doubles partner turned out to be a lanky guy from Arles. In his late twenties, he bore an uncanny likeness to Jesus, or at least the version that appeared in my children's picture books.

You know the sort: shoulder-length blondish wavy hair, ice-blue eyes, and a measured manner. Unlike Jesus, he happened to speak only French and, most importantly, he was a very handy tennis player.

Over the first weekend in August, we proceeded to demolish the opposition. I don't want to sound superior, but this didn't amount to much. I suppose better players had more sense than to play in temperatures that rarely dipped below 35 degrees. We found ourselves in the final beneath a blistering sun late on a Sunday afternoon. In this match, the best of three sets, we triumphed. Tearing off our headbands we sped to the net to triple-kiss our foes, as you do (whatever the gender) in this part of France. There was a gentle ripple of applause from assorted guests, which became more vigorous when *l'apéro* appeared. This is something *Provençale* folk do so well.

Throughout the weekend, families and friends had come to support their teams, watching from a grassy bank that bordered the court. The numbers had ebbed and flowed but now all the onlookers and players gathered in a closing picnic. Boxes of wine and bottles of pastis were passed around, and short eats were shared. The good-humoured hubbub was brought to a climax with prize-giving, chaired with genial aplomb by the club president. What touched me was the way everyone was honoured: runners-up, first-round losers, and even single red roses presented to some of the older ladies for just being there. Local enterprises generously sponsored the prizes – although I must admit I never did redeem my go-kart voucher. Returning home that evening I was again floating, this time on a wave of wine-soaked goodwill.

Beneath my laid-back exterior, there lurks a strong desire to out-do those around me… How refreshing it is then, to encounter a kingdom of understated soft power.

Amazingly, history repeated itself in two successive annual tournaments. Jesus' hair got a little longer each year, and my ability to understand his very fast, mumbled French did not improve, but still, we won through and bathed in *bonhomie*. Then the following year the tennis club committee changed. Out went the family-friendly, laid-back, extended picnic approach, and in came a more austere and competitive affair presided over by *Monsieur le Président* and a cadre of his club underlings. In name, it was the same *tournoi*, the same court but there had been a definite change in ambience.

My evidence for this had nothing to do with our inferior performance and lack of silverware, you understand. First, we were timed out of a match which we were narrowly losing with no 'five minutes to play' announcement. It transpired that we were playing the president's son and partner. Very convenient. The next year we came up against the president himself, Pierre, in the quarterfinals. In my first service game, the officious tone became obvious. His partner exclaimed '*Faute de pied*!'

Perhaps my toe had encroached a centimetre or two over the baseline, but let's not get too picky. After all, this was a social event, played for fun in a backwater village, wasn't it?

Well, it seemed not. As I served to his deuce court partner, Pierre stood as close to the net as he could and almost on the centre line, presumably to intimidate me. My serve swung with speed to the corner of the box, only to ping off his head into the 'stands'. I stifled a laugh and apologised. Jesus smiled. Pierre was none too pleased and took the point which was, very arguably, ours.

After a tense match, we were victors and shook hands. No companionable kisses, but rather a distinct feel of *froideur* at the net. We were in the semi-finals with a good chance of regaining our championship status in what had now become – in my fevered mind – an upmarket gladiatorial event, played for prizes. But the new regime had the last laugh. Not having my specs with me, I misread the continental timing of the next match and arrived 15 minutes late. The verdict of the organizing committee, sitting stern-faced at their folding table, was never going to be in doubt. '*Disqualifié!*' Sylvain was characteristically cool about the situation and sought to mollify my indignation. Indeed, he was far more Jesus-like than me.

There is a post-script to my tennis exploits. It was August 2020. Sylvain and I reunited to play in the local tournament once again. Having won through in the earlier rounds we faced a couple of middle-aged upstarts from a neighbouring village in the final. They boasted branded kit, bronzed limbs, designer shades and flashy rackets. 'All show,' I mumbled to myself as we wished each other *bon match*!

A storm had passed through at lunchtime leaving behind a duffle-coat of humidity and a slightly slippy court surface. I was absurdly tense so my serve went to pieces, my new medication for angina was just kicking in, and my partner – Jesus – must have been on something, too. It was not going to be our day and we slid slowly, defiantly, but irresistibly to defeat. In the final game, I stumbled while stretching for a backhand drive (just like the one on our bookcase) and crumpled in an ignominious heap. 'He's throwing the match' some sceptical onlookers muttered. 'Non, eez throwing eemzelf around like ze Boris Becker,' others countered.

'It's the drugs', April thought.

My boyhood fantasy of playing on Wimbledon's hallowed courts with an adoring crowd chanting my name was reduced to a match on the dirt-clay of a forgotten French village. The sprinkling of spectators was preoccupied with pizza and pastis. The match was over. No trophy again although we went up to graciously to receive our runners-up gifts: very natty face towels (I think that's what they were). The rest of the summer was spent with my left wrist in a protective sleeve to correct the dislocation. I might have pretended to be an archer looking for his bow or a falconer on his day off. But no one would have been fooled. To passers-by, it presented a chance for them to bore me with their own past injuries. For me, it served as a renewed emblem of imperfection: the humbling gap between what I aspired to in my imagination and what I was. In sport, as in other misadventures, perhaps it was time to leave the floating to others. To let my fellow competitors, even the French, win.

Was this whole debacle another clue about kingdom living? Writing to the church at Corinth, Paul remarks that *'the kingdom of God does not consist in talk but in power.'* (1 Corinthians 4:20). We live in a world of constant chatter, regaled with non-stop news, influencer opinions, and me-too campaigns. Most unsolicited. Much of this noise promises better connections, stronger friendships, improved health, and so on. Sometimes I feel like I'm trapped in a tunnel of talk. A persuasive voice in this echo chamber, from an early age, has been the urge to compete and be the best version of myself. This has entailed chasing the next gold medal and winning at whatever I do. It's ridiculous but difficult to resist.

So modest wins like at the village tennis tournament in a northern Provence village, give me bragging rights. Until I lose of course. How refreshing it is then, to encounter a kingdom of understated soft power where the last are first, servants lead, losers win, the least are honoured and children outshine adults.

8

SOMETHING FROM NOTHING MYSTERY

In France, the grape-picking harvest is called *la vendange du vin*. It is soaked in history and rooted in a region, a domaine. It requires collective action, the call to friends to come and help with the harvest. The encounter with the vines, with the soil, and with each other, is intimate. The flavour takes months to mature, but when it comes, many tastes dance on the palate and the vintage lingers long in the cellar. Sometimes for decades.

Around 15 years ago we were introduced to Emmanuel and his wife Erica in the *Cotes de Rhone* region of France. A biologist working in a Lyon hospital Emmanuel changed direction to take over his father's vineyard. The more relaxed lifestyle – with occasional bursts of intense activity – suits him well. Indeed, longevity is all but guaranteed. A glance at the label on his wine bottles shows the list of a family going back nine generations to the 1650s, all of whom lived to their nineties and some beyond. On our first visit to their *cave*, Romain served us chatting fondly about his prized vintages as if they were his children. Commendations and gold medal certificates were pinned proudly to the low beams. Having sampled a range of reds, we were on to the brandy (a spirit distilled from the fermented fruit mash) and about to settle up when Emmanuel appeared and graciously took over the payment.

'My father is getting a bit forgetful,' he told us quietly, 'sometimes he charges double, sometimes half, so it is well that I am around.'

Most of the grape harvesting is done mechanically by long-legged tractors, but Emmanuel always reserves one field for hand-picking. We've helped out on several occasions. In mid to late September, once the rain has given growth and the sun has ripened the crop, we get a call:

'...this Saturday morning at 8 am... Erica's field'.

This is one of the precious memories in my joy bucket. Each of us is given a literal bucket and a pair of secateurs. Arriving early in the morning, we join a group of pickers. They come from far and wide and there is an immediate sense of *camaraderie* as we work our way along the rows of low-hanging vines. Sometimes the work is silent, almost meditative, and sometimes there is good-natured banter. I join in the laughter, even if I sense that as a non-European Brexiteer, the joke is at my expense.

Large plastic buckets are filled quickly and tipped into a large bin towed by the tractor. Within minutes my hands are sticky with grape juice and the odd cut where I've snipped my fingers rather than the vines. The sun climbs in a cloudless sky, heating our backs while we bend low. Some bunches are as long as my arm. It feels good to ruffle the tendrils and foliage of the vines, smell the warm earth and handle the fruit. We are glad of the morning break, sprawling out on the grass with coffee and croissants in the shade of a mountain oak.

By mid-afternoon, my muscles are aching and my hands are a mess, but we are nearing the end. The tractor bins are full and we trudge back to the farm. They are tipped into a huge hopper with a large screw at its base. There are smiles of relief and satisfaction as we peer in, watching the stems and storks get separated from the grapes. Dark juice spurts into large hoses which snake their way to the vats inside. Emmanuel holds high a test tube and announces the sugar content is perfect. It is destined to be a splendid harvest. Customers across Europe will be relishing the subtle vintage of the fruity Grenache and the more complex Syrah for years to come.

There is a call to friends to come and help with the harvest. The encounter with the vines, with the soil, and with fellow pickers, is intimate.

Tradition has it that the pickers volunteer but are rewarded with a meal at the end of the day. We gather wearily and expectantly at the farmhouse for drinks and aperitives beneath a gnarled walnut tree. I begin to wonder whether I have misread the ritual. There is no hurry, no food, no sign of impatience. Then we amble into the cool space of the wine cellar where a long trestle table is laid. Still no sign of Erica. Finally, she comes from the kitchen bearing home-cooked beef stew, hunks of baguette, and platters of local cheese. The table begins to sigh with the ample portions, and I relax, chiding myself for having doubted the reward. A mix of languages flows as freely as the wine and the harvest is toasted more than once. There is a tinkling of glass as the bent and wiry frame of Romain shuffles to his feet. His speech is short but passionate, an exhortation to keep this tradition of hand-picking at least one field of grapes each year. The applause is sincere and respectful. After years of informal mentoring, it feels like the *vigneron* baton is being passed from father to son.

At one point, Emmanuel notices that the glasses are emptying. In one slow, deliberate movement and without looking back, he reaches behind his head for the bottles on the wine rack which he knows are there. Glasses are refilled with the fruit of his signature vintage. It is that small movement, which speaks of generosity, gratitude, of reliance on nature's bounty, that I recall most vividly as I think of the grape harvest in France.

As he sits back and surveys the scene in front of him, I wondered if Emmanuel knows his name means 'God with us'? and that he is living proof of a kingdom principle: *'The kingdom of God is as if a man should scatter seed upon the ground, and should sleep and rise night and day,*

and the seed should sprout and grow, he knows not how.'
(Mark 4: 26)

As city folk spoilt for commodity choice, with instant access to utilities and the anonymity of hypermarkets, April and I find it instructive to experience French rural life: deep furrows rather than skimming the surface. Enjoying the aroma and flavour of fruit and vegetables, locally sourced and only in-season; respecting and nurturing indigenous plant species rather than importing far flung varieties; valuing tradespeople who are proud of their *metier*, their job or craft, and won't deviate from it (unlike the British jack-of-all-trades); and winemakers like Emmanuel who tend their wines with fatherly care, allowing ample time for fermenting, distilling and maturing. None of this can be hurried and some of the best vintages are those that have spent the longest in the cellar.

The mystery of organic growth is nowhere better illustrated than in the vineyards of southern France, and my hero in this regard is Emmanuel. His wine cellar is rustic, his manner is gentle, and his farm is adorned with an eclectic mix of ancient agricultural implements. And, like so many in his profession as an organic farmer, he is utterly dependent on the nutrients of the soil, the vagaries of the climate, and the vigilance of the workers ('rising night and day') to produce rows of vines which, by mid-autumn, cascade with ripened grapes. What a wonderful picture of God's kingdom: us doing our bit and him doing the rest.

9

ULTIMATE SECURITY

Some days start with a feeling of exuberance when all is well. Like butterflies, we gad about in our freedom, our wings adorned in mottled hues of scarlet or speckled white. We flit from flower to flower without a care in the world, sucking nectar from the heavily scented hedgerows of plenty – oblivious to all. Until we catch sight of something sinister. Perhaps a spider or a hunter's net?

Within moments, our cherished liberty is gone. We are lassoed and immobilised. Skewered by arachnid fangs or pinned onto the green baize of a collector's pin-board. Removed from our joyous natural habitat. Displaced from where we belong.

Such was this day.

Staying at our French house for a couple of months each year meant I could occasionally combine pleasure with my professional work. I was taking a train from Valence in northern Provence to Spain. It was 2005 and we were midway through a European Commission research project with six partner countries. As principal investigator, it was my job to arrange for a different team

61

member to host a meeting every four months. And this time it was the turn of the Spanish partner. We were due to gather at his business school – in Barcelona.

Scurrying for my train at the ultra-modern station of Valence, I suddenly realised I'd left our French home without my passport. 'Will this be a problem?' I shot a question at the guard. He scanned my appearance and ticket dolefully. I was departing French borders, not arriving in the land of liberty, fraternity and egalitarian fervour to cause him trouble. He waved me through.

I settled into my seat with the air of a seasoned traveller. Academic work can be a thankless slog, but rare perks like this made it worthwhile. This was where I belonged. And, freed from the anxiety about the passport, I was looking forward to a leisurely evening meal with the team that night. Congregating from different cities, we could relax together before getting down to business the following day.

Effortlessly and on time, we pulled away. For anyone who used British trains regularly, it was immediately obvious that the French invested heavily in rail travel in the 1970s and 1980s, while the UK did not. Where Britain's outdated rolling stock still rumbled through tea-spilling junctions and points, France's high-speed TGV trains purred noiselessly toward their destinations. As we sped south, the hillside vineyards of Provence gave way to the wilder, flatter Camargue. The gentle sway and tilt of our streamlined capsule, the thrum of trees passing by at speed, and the low hum of foreign conversation soon had me dozing.

A little later as I shielded my eyes, the majestic Pyrenees came into sight, and we were chasing the setting sun.

Up in the hills nestled Céret. We had visited this small Catalan village a few years before. Back at the turn of the last century, Frank Burty Haviland took up residence to experiment with Cubism. It soon became a magnet for painters and sculptors attracted by the chance to meet fellow artists-in-residence. There was no obligation to pay rent, they were simply asked to donate a piece of their art as a departing gift. Just off the shady central square, we had come across a nondescript apartment block. It looked pretty ordinary, but the interior had been transformed into a stunning museum of art. Room after room of priceless exhibits featured works ranging from Dali to Matisse and Braque to Miro. Picasso was a frequent guest and among the gifts he left, which I admired greatly, were a series of animal sketches. Each was drawn in a single uninterrupted line. Such economy of effort, such lively simplicity. Such a lucky, talented bohemian.

The Med was easily visible along parts of the westerly route... and as the early evening light danced on the sea, I was reminded of camping holidays at Argeles Sur Mer, France's last big resort before Spain. Those were the days in the 1990s when we as a family would take off for two or three weeks in the summer to live under canvas. Windsurfers zoomed along the beach, swishing and tacking effortlessly. Later we watched an impromptu 'live show' as a bunch of French teenagers gathered to organize an indefinable beach game. Endless discussions over rules, flags, and teams, accompanied by arm-waving and Gallic shrugs from bronzed boys and a gallery of girls, posturing with poise. We never did see the outcome. Maybe *'badinage sur la plage'* was the actual game all along.

It was as we progressed into the foothills of the Pyrenees, with the setting sun turning the mountain peaks to the colour of bruised fruit, that I noticed a slight stiffening of mood. Into the carriage came a couple of uniforms. Their shiny leather holsters and fancy epaulettes suggested they were not TGV guards. Row by row they checked papers courteously but with minimum conversation. My turn came and I gave my *I'm not sure what you want but I'm innocent* look. For as long as I can remember, the appearance of police, even the sound of sirens, had always brought on an irrational sense of guilt. A feeling that transferred a shiftiness into my demeanour which was difficult to mask.

Mercifully, they moved on and I breathed easily again. The train passed through a tunnel and slowed. Some passengers began to gather their belongings as it seemed we had crossed the border. We were pulling into our first Spanish station. So far, so good. I knew who I was, where I was going and where home was. I rested easily in the comfort of these credentials. Much like a butterfly.

Portbou is a small, unassuming station up in the hills, yet the TGV halted here as it was a border point. Barcelona would be our next stop. Tapas and a glass of *manzanilla* beckoned.

Then, the uniforms returned. How swiftly things could change. With a jerk of their chins, they pointed me to the carriage door. A heap of defensive phrases fell into my head.

'You do realise that this is a career choice you are making here?' 'Can't you see that I am an English professor on my way to an important conference?' 'Look, I even have a crumpled Panama hat to prove it.'

But in my state of heightened anxiety, none of these mental pleas arrived at my mouth in anything resembling French, indeed anything coherent at all. With nonchalance flaking from me as fast as the batter from *gambas gabardina* (Spanish prawns in a raincoat), I alighted from the train. Of course, I could have stood my ground and demanded a phone call to the British consulate. But I didn't want to cause a scene. And, anyway, they had revolvers, and I only had a satchel. With a melancholy moan of the whistle, the train pulled away from the platform. This time without me.

Other travellers melted away and I found myself in the shabby station office with a rather ramshackle and downhearted family. I counted seven of various ages, from baby to grandparents, and it transpired they were from Bulgaria. They were waving a single paper document at the uniforms as if this would transport all of them seamlessly across the border. Only now was it dawning on me that this whole debacle was a matter of identity. Although without my passport, the guard at Valence had waved me onto the train, no doubt assuming I possessed a French national identity card. This piece of plastic with a photo is non-compulsory but with it, you can open a bank account, check in at a hotel, and travel with immunity. However, without it and having no identification on me, I was – in the eyes of the authorities – stateless. Without rights, an alien. Patently I did not belong.

As dusk descended on the near-deserted station, they continued to interrogate the Bulgarians and ignore me. I had plenty of time to think. Perhaps not in the most rational manner, it must be said. I observed the SNCF plaque screwed above the ticket office. Eventually, I

As dusk descended on the near-deserted station, they continued to interrogate the Bulgarians and ignore me... the big station clock with Latin numerals struck nine...

worked out that this denoted *Société Nationale des Chemins de fer Français*. What could be more comforting and solid than 'the French community of iron pathways', I muttered to myself. Then I noticed that the *SNCF* emblem was followed by *Réseau*. My dictionary revealed this to be a net, as in a spider's web, or *réseau berbeles*, a barbed-wire entanglement. Swiftly, I changed my focus to something less military and more hope-inducing.

Did I not recall that the *Entente Cordiale* was an Anglo-French agreement signed a century before? A couple of globally dominant colonial powers reached a joint understanding of who owned what, with a few clauses about fishing rights. Albeit in the distant past, surely the case of a forgetful English academic stranded on the Spanish border could be sorted with a swift and cordial handshake? This more promising line of thinking evaporated a little later. As the big station clock with Latin numerals struck nine, the uniforms reappeared and with a distinct absence of *badinage*, we were ushered into the back of a van. The vehicle looked like and bore the odours of, a black Maria. I recalled the black Madonna that I had once filed past in Montserrat's monastery. If she saved me now, I vowed, I would happily become a Catholic. The Bulgarians were still protesting, and my stomach was rumbling, but the dominant thought was which detention centre were we heading for?

Thirty tense minutes and as many hairpins later we were summarily disgorged into the square of a coastal town which I later discovered to be Cerbère. We had been deposited back in France. I was once again a free man, but hungry and tired. A small fishing port with a tiny beach, this appeared to be a picturesque out-of-the-way cove for holidaymakers. The Hôtel Le Belvédère looked smart and appealing but there were no rooms available. As I approached other bars and less chic hotels the shutters were rattling down for the night. Further down the coast, in Barcelona, the Spanish restaurants would just about be opening. But not here. My options were disappearing fast. At just after ten, when I should have been tucking into a plate of *buccaneros* in a bar off Las Ramblas, I was chewing a tasteless takeaway in the windowless back room of a motel.

Twenty-four hours after leaving, I was back precisely where I started at Valence. I had been nowhere and achieved nothing! But was the abortive journey entirely wasted? Certainly, I learned again, to be more careful with documentation especially when travelling abroad. Tetchy moments with the Italian *carabinieri* – the motorcycle police of Tuscany – and a missed flight to New York due to an absent passport should have taught me my lesson. It got me thinking about something a bit deeper. Having a grounded sense of where I truly belong.

During those hours in the station building at Portbou, with the grandfather clock ticking and the dark closing in, I had plenty of time to ponder this. I knew who I was: a British citizen in France trying to enter Spain. But I couldn't prove it. No amount of argument and righteous remonstration was going to convince the stone-faced authorities. No papers meant no citizenship. I was in the same boat as the Bulgarians who had somehow managed to slip across countless European countries only to be skewered at the Spanish border. It was a humbling place to be, and I felt in the pit of my stomach what it must be like to be a stranger, an alien. Yes, unlike countless other displaced people, asylum seekers, and refugees my plight was momentary, and I had a house to return to. Being manhandled by all this disappointment was only fleeting, but it gave me a glimpse of not belonging, of being in 'no man's land'.

As for the conference in Barcelona, the tapas and the theorising, it went ahead without me. Few of my colleagues believed my excuse. After a half-life of moving towards the middle, the limelight, the influential, was this another case of being eased from the centre of things? I felt gently chastened on several levels. I was stupid to travel without the required documents, it was embarrassing to be removed from the train at the Spanish border, and it was humbling to be driven by the police and deposited back across the French border. What was most disconcerting was feeling powerless and unable to use words to argue my case. Much as it is for millions of stateless people every day.

The author, in chapter 11 of Hebrews, refers to kingdom children as strangers and exiles on this earth who *'desired a better country, that is a heavenly one...a kingdom that cannot be shaken'* (Hebrews 12:28). Despite adversity, sometimes extreme and often to the point of death, a noble list of men and women are listed as a shining legacy for future generations. Living at different times and facing varying levels of stress, one thing unified them. Each hung onto their belief in God and the hope of being with him one day. And a bit like the artists in Céret, they had each left behind a gift that is still being talked about centuries later.

10

ALL OR NOTHING

Our youngest daughter, Mala, had fallen in love. Although her fiancé had not yet passed *his* initiation into the family – namely, participating in a tricky task with enthusiasm – a wedding for our fourth daughter, to follow her three older sisters, was on the cards. She expressed her desire to have the wedding take place at a local church in France to be followed by the reception in the garden of our home there. Having dreamt for many years of using our house and the gorgeous surroundings for such an event, I needed no persuading. Mala was keen to have a laid-back meal beneath parasols invoking the informal *Dejeuner des Canotiers* style of Renoir's famous painting. On closer inspection, it shows the men in singlets and straw hats quaffing wine with women folk looking up at them adoringly. I'm not sure that was quite what she had in mind.

Nestled in the heart of Manas, our nearest small village, is a small Catholic chapel. At one time packed for mass on Sunday mornings, the congregation has dwindled and for a while now, the building has been available for hire. It is an excellent acoustic space for choral concerts and other social events. At different times in its millennial history, it has been the official rallying point for the Pope's faithful, and an outpost of the Abbey run by the Bonlieu brothers, taking their statutory tithe of wheat and wine of course. In the twelfth and thirteenth centuries, it was a centrepiece of the garrison town, providing spiritual and physical succour for the Knights Templar. It must have felt a sweet haven as they returned weary and wounded from the Crusades, having battled Saladin for the Holy Land. The path over the mountains from Poet Laval and Eyzahut was well trodden by these warrior monks, heralded as heroes by some but reviled as bloodthirsty by many.

Seeking permission for the wedding required some careful steerage through ecclesiastical niceties. The Catholic sisters at the Poet Laval convent needed reassurance that an 'official' Protestant would be present (fortunately we had one by dint of our near neighbour being treasurer of a local church). The mayor of Manas hinted at a generous donation for use of the chapel and the French authorities required a complex set of documents and witnesses. We buckled at this last hurdle. Too much to do in a short space of time. The engaged couple secured their marriage certificate at a UK registry office and waited for the French church service a few days later to start married life together. Once all these details had fallen into place, along with choosing a minister (this was his first wedding), songs, readings, and a band, we felt we could relax a little.

Sitting in the cool of the chapel a week before the big day, I breathed slowly and absorbed the simple and unfussy atmosphere. For all its chequered past, stillness and tranquility seemed to chant from the rough-hewn stones. I was struck by the deep cobalt blue of the apse which radiated a sense of royalty and holiness. Apparently, in the recent past, the interior of the church had been restored by local benefactor Jacques Payan.

I later heard that he was the owner of several chateaux, and had built his fortune from, of all things, worms. Originally smuggled from China inside bamboo canes, this region of France established a thriving industry cultivating silkworms, nourished by the leaves from the plentiful mulberry trees. Once at their cocoon stage, they were boiled and strands of silk, up to several hundred metres long, could be pulled from the generous little creatures and woven into silk threads. From the specialist farms where this process took place, the silk was transported north to Lyon for the weaving of Jacquard material and south to Taulignon for the embroidery of episcopal vestments. Little is left of this lucrative cottage industry, except for merchants like Monsieur Payan. And it is thanks to him that this building where I was now sitting had regained its pride as a place of serenity. How uplifting when individuals share their wealth with the community.

A small fragment of the original wall colouring had been analysed and found to be a rare pigment used a thousand years before and later it became a treasured colour in the palette of Renaissance painters. It was the wish of Jacques Payan not to settle for second best but to recreate this stunning bold blue, providing a semi-circular backdrop to the altar and chancel. The story is also told that Jacques wished to restore the *lavoir* just

Nestled in the heart of Manas, our nearest small village, is a small Catholic chapel... Outside, April imagined cascades of white hydrangeas to greet wedding guests as they arrived.

across the street from the church. Again, seeking the best rather than making do, he traced the original source that had for centuries fed this public washing trough. It led to a spring 10 kilometres away. Methodically he secured the permission of all the respective landowners to pipe water along the route. Bar one, who with the true Gallic obstinacy of Magnon's neighbour in Pagnol's novel, resolutely objected. How strange, that Jacques Payan's wife was none other than the niece of Marcel Pagnol, the author who wrote with such drama about water in Provence.

My wife, April, has always had an eye for design. Her ideas for the flower displays were lavish and would have worked a treat in the damp, temperate climate of the UK. She chose massive glass containers filled with water and silver baubles as the basis of the formal displays at the front of the church. An assembly line of sisters and aunts created pew-end bouquets that shone in the drifts of sun that slanted in through high windows. Outside, she imagined cascades of white hydrangeas to greet guests as they arrived. The ambition of this entrance arrangement was admirable: a mere matter of throwing a rope over the high porch, weaving flowers to each side for a symmetrical display, and then, of course, keeping the whole thing looking fresh.

There were fraught journeys to and fro the evening before the service, with bundles of flowers, huge glass containers swaying on the back seat, and a bundle of rope. This had been carefully measured and cut to adorn the porch. As it turned out, we had miscalculated the lengths, so – to add to the drama – last-minute clambering on the porch roof was required to do some tying. Now and then we stopped to pick any extra greenery from the parched hedgerows. I was glad when it was so dark we could do no more.

Would the porch decorations still be there in the morning? Would they have wilted in the sauna heat? Would guests notice our painstaking handiwork as they were swallowed into the relative cool? According to my phone, the heatwave was set to continue the next day. We were in the middle of a *canicule*, translated as 'the hot period between early July and early September, a period of inactivity.' As in *cain*, dog day.

Brian, who helped us with the garden, retained his hippy ponytail despite approaching 80. Due to a bad back, he could only manage jobs between waist and shoulder height, which left a lot of low weeding and high pruning for me to do. One day he let it be known he'd spent 17 years – on and off – 'doing up' a special edition 1972 convertible VW beetle. He'd found it under layers of dust and bird poo in a local barn. Now bright red with gleaming chrome, he had taken his time doing a meticulous renovation job, although his first attempt to hand paint the bodywork had not been a success. Daring to exploit his shy pride I asked him one day:

'Would you drive my daughter and me to the church?'

'Well, I'm not sure...there are one or two things still to fix.'

'It's only a short distance. It would be great for photos.'

Brian searched the middle distance for another excuse: 'I've got nothing to wear.'

'Don't worry, I can lend you a white shirt.'

'Hmmm, I suppose I do have some old cricket flannels.'

As the big day in August approached, the excitement grew and the temperature cranked up to sauna conditions. Much time was spent tying up sails to trees in the garden to create pools of shade, outdoor lights were strung up, Mala hired a funky swing band from Lyon and discussions were held with Jérôme, a local *traiteur*. Having starred as a restaurant chef, this was to be his first outing as a commercial caterer, and he produced a stunning three-course menu for 50 or so guests. On the day of the wedding, we left him and his team to set up in our kitchen and packed the fridges with local *Clairette de Die* champagne.

Mala was hoping her good friend Rachel was making progress on her epic journey. She had left a dance workshop in Finland early that morning, with lightning changes from plane to Marseilles, train to Aix-en-Provence and a car pick up at Avignon.

Brian, looking splendid in his whites, duly arrived to transport us, ribbons streaming from the mirrors. I revelled in the gentle 10-minute drive to the church. What could be better than being chauffeured in a classic car with the hood down, my youngest daughter at my side, and the sunflowers of Provence smiling at us as we purred through country lanes? It mattered not that there was nobody around, this was part of the Drôme dream. By mid-day, Brian's temperature gauge was registering 36 degrees. As we parked under a tree by the church, a car pulled up with a spurt of dust. Rachel tumbled out, beaming and straightening her dress which she had changed into on the train. Mala briefly embraced her in relief and love.

Having secured the flowers in her hair, I walked the bride, who was brimming with grace, down the aisle. The orders of service had become fans, the floral displays may have lasted another hour before wilting and the guests about the same. For all the transience of nature, the eternal sacredness of the service touched us all.

On one occasion Jesus remarked to his followers: *'No one who puts his hand to the plough and looks back is fit for the kingdom of God.'* (Luke 9:62). When I read this aspect of kingdom living, it feels like an archaic and slightly harsh image. But on reflection, the message is bang up to date. We make promises today and break them tomorrow, we add clauses to contracts just in case, we qualify our commitments to cover a shift in circumstances. But this is not the way of the kingdom. With God, there is no turning back lest I swerve off course. No heeding the voices of sceptics and cynics. I swallow hard as I attempt to give up all, but when I do so, it seems I gain everything. Life is fleeting and there is no room for regrets. Even with a surname like mine, vacillation has no place. Whether in a wedding service or anywhere else for that matter.

Fortunately, we had placed some *bidons* of iced water in the fridges, so as the wedding party arrived back at the house after church, the champagne was put on hold. Out of the corner of my eye, I noticed Brian ferrying the bride and groom back for what was meant to be a rousing welcome as the shiny red car pulled in. But guests were in thirst-quenching mode and the moment was missed by most. For all the build-up, the driver and his car had managed to unintentionally dodge the spotlight. Later at the reception, I saw Brian sliding along in a strange crab-like fashion with his back to the patio wall.

'What's the matter?' I enquired discretely.

'It's me cricket flannels,' Brian whispered, 'they're ancient and they're all torn at the back.'

Serving water ice cold at the start of the wedding reception was a smart move. Saving the sparkly stuff for a little later ensured the guests were not too squiffy to sit down to enjoy Jerome's slow-cooked leg of lamb. I stole a quiet moment to scan our unusually crowded front lawn, which was gradually being taken over by the welcome shade. It was a mêlée of family and friends of all ages from ninety-four-year-old Joan in her wheelchair, who promised me the last dance, to the children sporting crisp wedding outfits that were beginning to peel off. The relaxed chatter and bursts of laughter, the joining of two families at tables beneath the awnings, the young cousins playing with their wedding favours...in the end the day slipped by so quickly. But that delightful picture will stay with April and me forever.

And, for another reason entirely I was glad we were able to savour Jérôme's exquisite meal, given what subsequently took place.

The wedding meal concocted and served by local legend Jerome was his first, and tragically his only, outing with his newly formed catering business. His last hurrah. Four months later, just before Christmas, he died of a massive heart attack. He was only in his early 40s. I recall that his entrée for the wedding had been *flan des courgettes sur un gazpacho et tuile de parmesan*. I imagine those slivers of toasted parmesan hoisted like wafer sails, as frail and tasty as life itself, bearing the memory of his flamboyant character to the hereafter. It was a timely reminder of the fragile division between earth and heaven.

Choosing to be married in the next village and celebrate with family and friends in the garden of our French house, our lovely daughter and fiancé made lifetime, indeed eternal, vows. Hesitation and caution in the early days of their friendship had given way to the unreserved commitment of devoted love. This is the kind of straight-line, no-looking-back, all-or-nothing abandonment asked of kingdom followers.

11

CLOSER THAN
YOU THINK

The purchase of a home in France is a wonderful dream come true. A place to take breakfast on the shade-dappled terrace, gaze at the changing hues of the distant mountains, sample the exquisite menus of hidden-away restaurants, to amble along the worn flagstones of medieval villages. In the summer it becomes a hostel for our extended family (now 20 in number), a place to welcome friends for unhurried meals with fine wines beneath stars that seem so close. Yet alongside the ideal, the real often breaks in. The costly repairs, the unending taxes, the rampant weeds, the moaning mistral, all take a turn in elbowing the dream aside for a while.

One of these unwanted intruders is poor health. For a while I am fighting fit, brimming with energy, climbing mountains to see the sunrise from beneath me. Then comes physical pain or illness, or maybe degenerative disease. The world shrinks, horizons close in, and the question 'Why me?' hangs in the accusing air. And, particularly if one signs up, as I do, to faith in an all-powerful, compassionate, miracle-working God, his apparent absence is mysterious at best, and downright baffling at worst.

Sometimes the pain is minor and self-inflicted. Recently, I was removing obstinate turf from around the bases of our apricot, apple and cherry trees. In the Drôme, irrigation is essential as rain can be scarce in the summer months, apart from occasional thunderstorms when the heavens tear apart but the rain doesn't have time to soak in. It gushes away to soggy ditches and parched riverbeds. I was checking the pipes and nozzles of our *goutte* à *goutte* system and piling on some mulch, kept in place by heavy stones. My back protested and gave way. Spartacus, from being a rebel gladiator, brandishing his sword to take on the might of Rome – or, in this case, the invasion of alien weeds – was reduced to Sciatacus, a feeble and anguished slave leaning on an old man's walking cane. It started as a stiff lower back, followed the next day by a shooting pain down the back of my left leg. The sciatic nerve, usually so reliable and silent, was crying out. I hobbled around, hopping from one piece of furniture to another, not daring to put weight on my left side.

I felt as helpless as a toddler learning to walk. I was humbled like a felled tree. So, when the apostle Paul breezily exclaims that when he is weak, that is exactly when he is strong[1], what can he possibly mean? He adds to this apparent nonsense by boasting about his weakness so that the power of Christ may rest upon him. There are several interpretations which I mentally rule out. This is not an invitation to wear our pain as a perverse badge of honour. Nor is it an exhortation to be very British by putting on a brave face (while inwardly grimacing). Nor is it a quasi-religious transaction whereby current suffering earns brownie points in some far-off future. I'm sure he doesn't mean that we should go looking for situations

---

1   2 Corinthians 12:9-10

that overwhelm us or seek reckless adventures to pile on the pain.

Apart from running a successful gite business, at the time Bob and Celia co-led a small house church up in the Drome hills and we joined them when in France. Perhaps they will have some answers? A group of families meeting in the cool of the shuttered lounge to sing, reflect and pray, receive teaching from whoever feels led, and then afterwards, under the wisteria on the patio, enjoy an expresso, sip *vin rosé* and sample a range of olive tapenades. This, for me, is what church should be: inclusive, family-oriented, informal, unpredictable, honest, whole-life. Given the various ailments we and those we love are facing, we were often pressing into God's heart for healing. Not for the first time over the years, we were studying how Jesus restored the health and sanity of those he encountered. The dissonance between these good news stories and the grim reality of illness and setbacks in our midst was unspoken but silently mocked like a fallen angel. Discussion was upbeat and self-pity scarce, but it was like we were congregating at the extreme end of a jetty of faith. It was creaking, in danger of collapse.

The question that had bothered me for years resurfaced. If God is so powerful, why don't we see him heal more often? At different times my answer has shifted from one foot to another like an innocent pupil summoned to the headmaster's office. Should I risk pleading my case for mercy for something I don't think I deserved? Or just take the rap?

In my younger days, I suppose I simply accepted what might be called the biological view. Yes, our bodies are incredibly intricate and well-balanced organisms, with highly sophisticated software, equipped to be durable and adaptable. For all that, they are prone to wear and tear, damage, and gradual demise. So, why bother God to intervene? Although he *can* supernaturally accelerate the process of healing and miracle-working, he chooses to operate mainly within the scope of the natural. The five senses he gave us. So best to leave healing to the physicians who have the expertise. Although God is capable of zapping like a microwave, an oven is the norm.

But then theology began to give biology a run for its money. Invariably Jesus spoke healing into people's lives, and they immediately regained sanity, well-being, sight, strength and the like. Then he asked his followers to do likewise. It was in that spirit that I, as a novice believer, prayed for my dad. Sceptical about God though he was, the pain in his back was so intense that he put aside his pride. One evening he asked his son to pray. Feeling thoroughly inadequate, I put my hands on his back and simply claimed some promises from my bible. The shooting pain (caused by a growth on his spine which was tweaking nerve ends) went and did not return. I was as surprised as my dad and took encouragement to pray for many others since. My success record since has been middling to below average. Why is that? I wondered.

I think of an English couple. Within a year of them starting a new life here in a nearby village in the Drôme, the husband contracted prostate cancer. It was diagnosed too late, and he died a slow, lingering death. Our little French band of believers prayed earnestly and often, apparently to no avail. It occurred to me that maybe we were becoming superstitious. Not in the sense of believing astrology or witches' incantations, but were we reducing healing to an unspoken bargain with God: 'If you heal this dear man, then we'll believe in you more'? Jesus was not impressed by those Jews who followed him just because of the 'magic' of miracles.

But also, perhaps my definition of 'success' was woefully human. From my child-like perspective, I wanted healing to be visible and immediate. Overlooking the fact that illness and pain are complex with many interconnected root causes of dis-ease: physiological, mental, emotional, and spiritual. I was learning that Jesus when he encountered sickness, dealt with people holistically. For him, physical well-being was just a part, he diagnosed and gave attention to the real – not the presented – needs. Sometimes he discerned the crippling grip of unforgiveness, or the heavy hand of legalism, or some kind of emotional shackle that needed release, or simply unbelief, that had to be dealt with first.

It was dawning on me that, somewhat mysteriously, God sometimes uses pain, including ill health, to get our attention. A bit like the 'gift' of our French house. He wanted me to live the dream but not to get distracted or beguiled by it. Rather, as with good health, he wanted me to hold it lightly. Might it be that God wanted nothing more than for me to turn voluntarily from the appealing, but far inferior, loves of my daily life to pursue him? For me to miss this invitation to find what my soul longed for – to love and be loved – was to miss everything. One way to give me this wake-up call to seek Him is via setback. Whether it be gnawing pain, the onset of a life-threatening disease or simply the cocoon of normal life unravelling. Into the darkness of this void, he whispers his comfort and draws alongside like an invisible but trustworthy companion.

What does our little group up in the Drôme hills do as we gather on the 'creaking jetty'? Imperfectly we continue to pray for healing and recovery from setbacks, believing that God hears and answers *every* heartfelt prayer, but in his sovereign way and perfect time. If God is God, and I know this is a big ask for many, he holds the universe in his hands. Surely, it follows then, he *can* arrest disease, he *can* re-create lost organs and, yes, he *can* extend limbs at will – and sometimes does. Yet in his eternal perspective, he often chooses to engage with us in ways far more profound, to accomplish things far deeper and more awesome than we can think or imagine.

Gradually I am coming to see suffering and setbacks in a fresh light. To see times of frailty as opportunities to wean me off self-sufficiency. To regard physical weakness as a signal of my spiritual neediness. To encourage me to place my confidence in more substantial things than my own strength, which inevitably depletes, and will ultimately disintegrate. I can't tell you how difficult this is. From an early age, I have been tutored to be emotionally resilient, to be robust in sports, to excel in my studies, and to perform well in my work. My experience at university (as a student and then later as a member of the faculty) has only served to heighten the importance of sounding competent. Unlearning all this takes time. Unwinding in France helps. I find myself coming back to Jesus who pioneers a more radical path. He asks me to embrace vicissitudes as part of my maturation as a mortal. He doesn't want me to suffer but allows it. He doesn't cause me harm, but He uses it. He doesn't wilfully rain down pain upon me but soaks my inner self, if I let him, with the resources to cope.

For the historical rebel Spartacus, the arena was public and heroic as he led a growing band of liberated slaves against a succession of Roman legions. For me as Sciaticus, the battle is far less glorious and more private. How – in the clutches of infirmity – do I rise above the slavish tendency to moan, to blame, to be defeatist? How do I find a way of believing that God is alongside me? And in control?

Back to my back. I had an appointment with the physiotherapist here in France. Twenty minutes passed in the waiting area and I was getting edgy at being ignored. I was getting used to waiting in French queues but the lack of acknowledgement that I was in the room still irritated me. Once my turn came, Jory, a smart young man the age of my children, gave me his full attention, explained the situation (possibly a slipped disc) and manipulated my body with compassion and skill. An hour later, the shooting pain in my left buttock and thigh had eased slightly as I limped across the scruffy clinic car park. The bright spring sunshine, elderly villagers sitting on wicker chairs outside their front doors, the smiling crocuses and primroses: all was normal and working as it should.... all except me. I could not help feeling gloomy at the prospect of enforced rest, exercise ('the Mackenzie method three times a day') and, maybe surgery. For all the religious theories – welcoming trials as friends and seeing the bigger picture – I still asked God 'Why me?' What, I inwardly ranted, has any of this to do with the health of my soul? Wordlessly, the answer came: 'Everything'.

Sometimes what I dream for seems far off. I struggle with the gap between where we are and where we want

The bright spring sunshine, elderly villagers sitting on wicker chairs outside their front doors...all was normal and working as it should.

to be. How can I ever attain the goals I set for myself, and the expectations of those around me? When others are apparently enjoying success, I get impatient and doubts creep in. Especially if ailments, poor health, and setbacks get in the way. Yet, flying in the face of this gloom, Jesus assures me that *'The time is fulfilled, and the kingdom of God is at hand. Repent, and believe in the gospel.'* (Mark 1:14-15). He seems to be whispering in my ear that his presence, his kingdom is very near, in our midst, within touching distance. How can that be?

The only answer I can come up with, improbable though it sounds to human ears, is that my earthbound existence with all the limitations of mortality can be eclipsed by another kingdom. Not in some far-off parallel universe, but right now. Right here. A 'location' where hope is not dependent on good health, where tranquility is rooted in trust, and well-being rises above adverse circumstances. Like the sciatica I succumbed to in France. This is no self-help maxim or positive thinking mantra. It comes from listening to a kingdom-bearer who has authority over disease and even death itself because, uniquely, he has been to the grave and back.

12

REVEALED
NOT DISCOVERED

For some people, dreams are illusory and escapist. A way of distracting us from the monotony or the stress of the present. Perhaps there was some of that when April and I first started visualising summers in France. We'd taken some lovely vacations under canvas in the Dordogne, the Cevennes and the south of France. The laid-back atmosphere, the long meals with fine wines under starlit skies, and the sumptuous scenery drew us back year after year. So, when the opportunity came to purchase a holiday house in northern Provence, a place where our burgeoning family could gather under one roof each summer, we needed little encouragement to pursue the dream. Albeit with some trepidation, we took a step of risk from the familiar to the far-out-there. On the face of it, this has little to do with an international particle physics experiment. But in the same way that I am picking over the debris of our collisions with French customs in the Drôme, the scientists at CERN pursue their professional dream by scrutinizing the debris of colliding particles.

On the 4th of July 2012, scientists at the Large Hadron Collider on the French-Swiss border clustered around the banks of computers in the control room. Incredibly, nearly fifty years after particle physicists first made their daring prediction, the so-called Higgs boson was discovered. After painstaking and precise observation of tiny particles, the debris of one collision indicated the presence of what they were looking for. At the same time a sister experiment, also at CERN but using different technologies, confirmed that their search was over. There was uncharacteristic emotion, shouting and high-fives as news flickered through on the screens. The relief and joy were reminiscent of NASA when Neil Armstrong stepped onto the surface of the moon.

Such a feat could only have happened with an international team of experts willing to cooperate over many decades. This is the so-called ATLAS experiment at the university campus near Geneva. The investigation centres on a cavernous 21-kilometre underground tunnel. Here particles are thrown at each other at just less than the speed of light. In 1964 a small group of particle physicists, including Peter Higgs and François Englert predicted that there was one vital piece missing in the jigsaw of theoretical physics. Namely what makes particles stick together. This elusive part of the jigsaw became colloquially known as the 'God particle' because, without this component, the universe would not exist in its current form. To fund the experiment, the governments of 38 countries contributed a huge chunk of their science budget year after year for a generation. The risks of being very publicly mistaken were huge. I once watched a TV interview with Peter Higgs. As the bushy-haired professor spoke to the camera I was glued to what he was saying for about half a minute, at which point he turned to the blackboard behind him and disappeared in a cloud of chalk dust and equations!

Not long after came an uncanny coincidence. I met Yvon Englert, the nephew of François Englert. We were walking our dogs on the track behind our French property. A rector at the Free University of Brussels and a specialist in gynaecology and obstetrics, he turned out to be our neighbour in France. On one occasion when he was showing us around his summer house in the woods, he pointed out some secret panels in the floorboards of the bedroom:

'Our Jewish family narrowly escaped Auschwitz in the war and my father has always been haunted by the experience. Ever since, wherever he went, he always incorporated these secret spaces. Just in case.'

I still feel a chill as I pass that house. It seemed that receiving the Nobel prize in 2013 (along with Higgs) prompted Francois Englert for the first time to go public with his harrowing story: his escape with his family from the Holocaust. A case of a fulfilled dream chasing away a persistent nightmare perhaps?

Pursuing dreams, or more simply, reducing the gap between 'what is' and 'what could be' has fuelled a lot of my thinking as an adult. As I pulled on my green apprentice overalls at a car assembly plant in the 1970s, I frequently asked myself why workplaces must be so dull and dispiriting. As a student, I was caught up in many social scientific utopias, but the theory rarely translated into practice. As a psychologist, I came across clear explanations of what was wrong with the human condition, but remedies were thin on the ground. As an academic, I surfed the wave of leadership studies – by far the biggest growth area in business schools – which seemed to offer some glimmers of light. But again, judging by the day-to-day ineffectiveness and dubious ethics of many leaders, this arena of promise also fell short.

Then one day, as I was in my study wading through papers and websites, I came across an organization that appeared to buck this trend by achieving an incredibly ambitious scientific goal against all the odds. I was keen to know more. Although particle physics was lost on me, I secured funding for a three-year research project to take a closer look at the way the physicists and technologists worked together on the ATLAS experiment at CERN. Coming from 175 Institutes dotted across the world, they appeared to collaborate well without language, culture, or technology getting in the way.

Through lots of interviews and observation of the way things happened at CERN, I began to see what it meant to dream. Sometimes the lessons were subtle, sometimes small, but always telling. On one occasion we were watching a large meeting taking place in a lecture theatre. A fault had developed in the Collider and from the dais at the front, the Coordinator was running through options. Keenly following her briefing, 150 physicists sat attentive with laptops open. The LHC accelerator was capable of producing billions of particle collisions a second, and from these, underground detectors tracked those with interesting trajectories. As I struggled to follow the figures being thrown around, I noticed the clocks on either side of the lecture hall. I smiled to myself. Here were super-scientists discussing figures like 10 to the power of 13 which would explain the beginning of the world. Meanwhile, both analogue clocks on the wall had long since stopped.

For me, it summed up a couple of things about dreaming. First the huge step of faith – or what they called 'stretch goals' – this experiment made in predicting the discovery of the Higgs boson amongst all those billions of collisions. And then, how this vision was not hampered by mundane details like wall clocks. I spoke to scientists who had staggered out of the computer room after a marathon shift, not knowing the time of day or whether the next meal was breakfast or dinner. Not to be commended perhaps, but it showed the passion of these physicists who were united by their intoxicating dream of discovering the missing particle.

Pursuing their dream was a shared and infectious endeavour. For all the intranet communications around the globe, it was clear that informal face-to-face gatherings were key. I recall my first visit to the huge cafêteria, located at the CERN campus. It was early-morning, and the place was already buzzing. Little groups were gathered around coffee tables. Several nationalities were engaged in animated discussions. It had the feel of a street bazaar where unusual ideas and juicy innovations were being traded freely and generously.

Although I didn't fully appreciate it at the time, this was something unique. An international research and development (R&D) collaboration united in their collective goal of explaining the last few milliseconds preceding the Big Bang. This was no trivial matter. The quest was to simulate how they believed the world came into being.

My research travels to and from CERN happened during the time we were pursuing our own dream: ingratiating ourselves into a French lifestyle. Although there is a huge difference between a global science experiment and our summers in Provence, I was beginning to discern something about the anatomy of dreams. Like

The dream hinges on the spontaneous hubbub of a 'bazaar'. ... the banter, the sounds and songs, the thrills and spills, and the variety of prize products found in a marketplace.

the scientists pushing the envelope of understanding, we were very much at our frontier of language and culture. At one level new knowledge is little more than information, freely available and coming at us from all directions. For the physicists, this was everyday data digitally stored in microchips and computer code. For us, it was language embedded in dictionaries and learning apps like *Duolingo*. However, such technologies only take us so far. There is a very different kind of know-how that occurs in 'aha' moments, sometimes referred to as tacit knowledge because it's invisible, not written down and we often don't know we have it! Here I think of the fluid discourse in CERN's *cafêteria*. Whereas for us as a family, it was tentative conversations in French where the flow suddenly clicked. Locals began to understand me and I felt great for a while until speedier speakers or thicker accents kicked in. Or times when the French way of life spoke back to me, like French children remaining at the dining table with their parents, participating in the repartee rather than hurrying away to play on their tablets.

The huge dedication of the scientists, the highly sophisticated equipment they are using, and the hyper-vigilance of their day-and-night observation are impressive, but it occurs to me that this is not how God's kingdom is apprehended. There are times when our reliance on logic, intellect, and mental effort alone can be a hindrance. No amount of intense observation, rigorous analysis and high fiving will bring the kingdom into being. This is because his kingdom is not discovered by men but revealed by God. It is not experienced out-there but illuminated in-here. Once again Jesus gives us the key: *'The kingdom of God does not come with observation; nor will they say, "See here!" or "See there!" For indeed, the kingdom of God is within you.'* (Luke 17:20-21).

There was a half-century gap between predicting and finding the Higgs' boson, which shows the virtue of sticking with the dream. But while a piece of knowledge like the

Higgs' boson may complete the model of applied physics, the scientists are the first to admit that there are mysteries in the universe yet to be explained. They are aware that the thrill of seizing the day or living the dream has a way of receding as new, bigger dreams come into view. It might be said that the history of science is one of constant realisation that what was once considered certain requires some modification. This demands humility. Einstein once said that: *Nature shows us only the tail of the lion. But I do not doubt that the lion belongs to it even though he cannot at once reveal himself because of his enormous size.* [1] The apostle Paul says something similar: 'Now we see but a poor reflection as in a mirror, then we shall see face to face. Now I know in part; then I shall know fully, even as I am fully known' (1 Corinthians 13:12).

Another thing that dawned on me as I loitered around the CERN campus was that dreams are not neutral. There are many examples of scientific discoveries motivated by committed and well-intentioned researchers, being misused by others for dubious or evil purposes. Realised dreams require fresh decisions. This may appear – especially to scientists – to be the territory of cold logic. Yet new knowledge implies a 'hot' choice. In our case, we were faced with questions like: how do we make our French property available to those not so well off? Do we opt for cheaper oil central heating or the more sustainable wood pellets? Do we take sides with our immediate neighbours or seek to be peacemakers? Mundane matters compared to the 'Big Bang' perhaps, but all dreams have a moral edge. Their realisation brings fresh responsibilities.

---

1   Pais, Abraham (2005) 'Subtle is the Lord...':The Science and Life of Albert Einstein, Oxford University Press, New York

Some may question the point of scientific experiments, and the huge investments by governments in such speculative activity. There is no guarantee of 'return'. There is a strong element of risk, of testing boundaries. We might even call it calculated non-conformity. A sign that allegedly hung on Einstein's office wall at Princeton put it well: '*Not everything that counts can be counted, and not everything that can be counted, counts.*' [2] As I witnessed at CERN, although the Large Hadron Collider is stunning in its technical complexity, in many ways the dream hinges on the spontaneous hubbub of a 'bazaar'. On the banter, the sounds and songs, the thrills and spills, and the variety of prize products found in a knowledge marketplace.

Again, I can see parallels, in a far humbler way, with our French adventures. It would have been safer, and more comfortable, to stay in our British bubble. But by investing time, energy, and funds in the dream of summers in France, committing *faux pas,* and teetering on a tightrope of cultural acceptance, we arrived at some of our own missing particles: benefits that were not always visible and could not be easily quantified; horizons that bit wider; friendships that bit richer; self-knowledge that bit deeper.

2   McCubbin, N (2011: vii) Collisions and Collaboration, eds Boisot, M, Nordberg, M, Yami, S and Nicquevert, B, Oxfors University Press, New York.

13

FREE ENTRY,
NO BAGGAGE

Along with around 86,000 other Brits, we have chosen France to set up a second home. For this privilege, I am extremely grateful. But actually getting there these days is proving to be an arduous and frustrating adventure. For two decades we have provided gainful employment to an array of trades (from roofers to electricians, from gardeners to builders), we have brought income to restaurants, local businesses, and vineyards, and we have pointed paying guests towards golf clubs, local markets, museums, and art galleries. We have dutifully submitted taxes, paid handsomely for the odd medical treatment, and contributed more than 4000 euros, thus far, to the upkeep of autoroutes via the *péage* (toll) system. Might we have anticipated a small measure of gratitude for bringing revenue into the area from Monsieur Macaroon (as he is referred to by many French)?

In 2020, thanks to our over-promising, bamboozling British PM, we second-home owners found ourselves excluded from Europe and the doors effectively shut on our own houses (and as one of those voting to leave I am especially galled). Unless studying abroad, married to an EU national, or having a constituted business in

France, we are apparently not welcome to stay more than three months. Or at least, that is the not-so-subliminal message. If this sounds harsh and a touch paranoid, let me introduce the game of *Francopoly*.

To enter the game you need to have a laptop and a credit card. Hard luck if you don't; without them you are a non-starter. The next rule is that you deal not with the French consulate but with a shadow, arm's length visa agency. Registering and logging into an account should be straightforward but took me the best part of a day. This is due to baffling internet instructions, opaque messaging, and telephonic dead-ends. When you *have* tracked down the elusive number to answer queries, you encounter call centre staff who rapidly descend from courteous to just curt. All part of the initiation of booking a place at the table.

Physical presence at the visa centre is a must. A two-hour rail journey to the other side of London seems justifiable if only to have some human interaction. This years' experience was especially frustrating. My wife's papers were intact but a small clerical error (shortening my name to Chris on one of the many documents) disqualified me at the first hurdle. No, I was not allowed to correct it there and then. *'Your application is now blocked and you have to return home and start the process again tomorrow,'* was the deflating instruction. Terms like inflexible and fastidious are some of the more polite words that came to mind. But then, I remembered I was entering the faceless recesses of French bureaucracy.

Regathering our strength, we decided to forge ahead with April's application and leave mine for another day. Perhaps forge is an overstatement. We joined a scrum of other applicants, playing vacantly with their phones. A long list of 8-digit numbers were displayed on multiple screens. Depressingly our number didn't appear for another half hour. It gradually crept to the top and finally, a bell rang for an open booth. It was now an hour beyond our original appointment time. The clerk wearily informed us that we hadn't photocopied the correct forms and that April's photo was *'only permissible for USA and India'* (as if one's appearance changes as you approach different borders) and my bank statement could not be used for two different criteria (proof of income *and* financial solvency). Despite these misdemeanours, the clerk stamped several forms with unusual force, and we were through! Well not quite, there was a matter of the service fee. Payable before we received any service and non-returnable in the case of a rearranged appointment or a withdrawn application. So, we had paid £60 so far for no service. Oh, and although it was originally designed to cover the mailing of completed visas, we were informed this had been suspended *'because too many passports were getting stolen'*. The service had been removed but not the fee.

The ordeal was not over. Another waiting room, another dawdling screen, and another disconsolate queue, this time for fingerprints and biometrics. We had this done at the same visa centre the year before, but either the records were irretrievable or such immutable personal data as unique fingerprints can evolve, making re-testing essential. After three hours, we emerge blinking into the characterless courtyard with the de-spiriting thought that I must go through all this again for *my* entry to France. Given that the passports containing our long-term visas can only be picked up by hand, that means four separate visits to winsome Wandsworth.

The difficulty of entry is down to me and the baggage I carry...
my desire to bring other stuff with me.

Collecting the visas entailed a swifter but no less bureaucratic battle. On arrival, I was informed that originals *and* photocopies were required for all forms. The photocopier at the centre was adorned with an 'out of order' sign, so, losing my place in the snaking queue, I was directed to a post office at the end of the street. The PO assistant was obviously geared up for this little side-line. A notice informed customers that copies cost 50p for black and white and £1 for colour. Conscious that we'd spent £90 each on the visas and £30 each for the non-existent service, I saw this as a token but symbolic act of taking back control. I chose the 50p photocopy. When paying, the cashier informed me with suppressed satisfaction that there was a minimum charge of £1. As I rejoined the queue at the visa centre, I couldn't help thinking how spot-on Kafka was. The nightmare of being crushed by nonsensical authority, of being enmeshed in a bizarre and impersonal administrative maze where you feel powerless to understand or control what is happening.

How similar yet different to entering the kingdom. In another of his cryptic comments, Jesus says: *'How hard it is to enter the kingdom of God! It is easier for a camel to go through the eye of a needle than for a rich man to enter the kingdom of God.'* (Mk 10:25). Unlike France, the problem is not maddening bureaucracy, financial payment, or obstructive rules. Indeed, in his love, God is passionate in wanting us to join him and enjoy his loving presence. The difficulty of entry is down to me and the baggage I carry. So many things can get in the way: my self-importance, my mixed motives, my sense of entitlement, and my desire to bring other stuff with me. Stuff that I hanker after and hang onto in this country but is not necessary or needed in his.

Armed with papers, passports, visas and photos, including a 13-page explanation from the vet concerning our dog's health (another post-Brexit regulation, this one costing £120), we finally made it through the French border control unscathed and set off for Drôme Provence. Lovely though our destination is, we do wonder whether a short-term stay will suffice in the future. I gather the number of Brits with French properties has dropped by a third. Surely it won't be long before TV producers turn this whole escapade into '*Celebrity, get me IN there*'.

I recognise that many struggle to own a *first* home in the UK, but for those aspiring to become second homeowners in France (or elsewhere in Europe) the hassle and costs are not to be underestimated. It requires navigation of a complex online system, lip-biting patience when dealing with contract staff, and perseverance in following the unhelpful and unyielding rules. Yet it occurs to me that even this frustration has perverse virtue. It is a process that cannot be rushed, there is no way of queue jumping, and it is a great leveller. Unlike the nepotism of some professional worlds I have inhabited, all are treated the same no matter what or who you are. There is no calling favours or preferential treatment, you cannot appeal to a higher authority. Taking me back to the colleague at the door of my university office (Chapter 2: Heaven on Earth), there is no referent power.

Fortunately, when it comes to the kingdom, entrance is open to all, and the invitation comes from none other than the King himself.

14

LED BY CHILDREN

It was never intended to be more than a one-off light entertainment evening during the 'family fortnight' at La Grange. 'Let's do a show,' the grandchildren pleaded, jumping up and down with excitement. In the first years, there were just a few of them, but now there are 11 with ages spanning nearly 20 years. It's an opportunity for them to take centre stage, to dress up in random gear (chainmail, studded belts and other punk-like props raided from Celia's alter ego wardrobe). A platform to tell good jokes badly, to learn some lines and to show off dance moves in front of the grown-ups. The last bit is important of course. The adults (a rent-a-crowd of parents with phone cameras rolling, invited friends and press-ganged passers-by) have their seats assigned by hand-made tickets. In return, they are expected to laugh in the right – or wrong – places and generally enter into the spirit with enthusiasm. In short, this is a rare chance for the kids to be in charge, although misbehaving in front of a captive gallery at mealtimes comes a close second.

Having got buy-in from the grown-ups and chosen the night, then comes the challenge of what to 'perform'. In the early days, I learned to anticipate that a show might happen, so sketched a few ideas before the families arrived. Stories from the bible seemed to lend themselves well to a multi-actor, action-packed, part-narrated adventure, so that's where I went for initial source material. Leading the grandchildren off to a quiet space, we'd start to storyboard the plot together. That sounds a bit grand, but at least we'd discuss the characters and try out a few punch lines. I have to say, this for me, was often the best bit: the kids clustering around, sharing ideas from their fertile imaginations, the plot morphing into a new animal altogether, some rising to the occasion, others storming off in tears, all teetering on the tightrope of their confidence. For all the setbacks, sulks and walk-outs, there was a burgeoning buzz through the week as show night approached, and by then everybody had at least a walk-on part to play, from the youngest to the oldest. Even the adults were nervous, knowing that they may be picked out to participate in some way likely to embarrass.

I recall one son-in-law, still adjusting to a full-on family holiday, who was chosen by the kids to play the scheming Haman. This was in a potted re-enactment of the Esther story from the Old Testament, where he – as a senior adviser to King Xerxes – was scripted to lurk in the background with a plastic bucket on his head to make him look important. Despite initial hesitation, he quickly grew into his role and was duly booed on each malevolent appearance. Meanwhile, another son-in-law – known to sing from lamp-posts but only at the end of a drink-filled evening – played a creditable and sober king. Stealing the show was the grand-daughter role-playing Esther, whose renowned beauty made her number one in the harem. More panto than serious play.

It wasn't long before her aptitude for the stage showed itself. Her compering of Strictly Come Prancing, was priceless, introducing various cousin-couples as they swooped and swirled before two rows of adult judges. In the first post-Covid year, she excelled as MC while doubling, backstage, as wardrobe manager, prompter, props organiser and music maestro. By this time, I was doing very little on these shows which have become an annual fixture. The kids have taken over with aplomb.

hiding seek 2015

They want to be found and sometimes they make little squeaking sounds, just to guide the catcher towards them.

For all the board games, outings to the local river and special treats, the one game that our grandchildren never tire of playing is hide and seek. And the garden in France is spacious enough to provide lots of scope for 'secret' places. There are squeals and a frenzy of commotion as the children scatter while one person buries their face and counts to 30. Peeping through their fingers of course.

Little feet race to familiar hiding places. At first not far away, perhaps behind the hedge or tight against the lime tree. The very same place they went before. It's almost as though they dare not venture further.

They want to be found and sometimes they make little squeaking sounds just to guide the catcher towards them.

Over time, they get more adventurous and find more daring hiding places. There they wait, holding their breath, in a state of nervous anticipation as footsteps approach. It's a strange mix of feelings that I can remember as a child: revelling in the cleverness of concealment and yet slightly scared that we might be missed. Because *not* to be found is a huge letdown. On occasions, a little one hides so well that no one discovers their secret hidey-hole. The game finishes and they remain alone, sometimes for a long time before their absence is noticed. *Oh, how could they overlook me? Where has everybody gone?* The heightened trepidation of evading capture quickly ebbs away. In its place, disappointment rushes in followed by a minor meltdown because they've been forgotten.

Is this, I wonder as I reflect on my spiritual journey, a bit like me and God? There have been times when I delighted in leaving him counting, as I scattered from his presence. I got better and better at hiding over the years, sometimes daring myself to go further and further from where I left him. The exhilaration of finding nooks and crannies, where I think I am out of sight to do as I please. My heart palpitates as I hear his footsteps approaching and I hold my breath as his shadow passes. *Where are you?* He calls out in a gentle voice. I congratulate myself on remaining undetected. Time passes. Just as I start thinking he has forgotten me, He returns. He pulls away my cover and gathers me up in his arms. My perspiring pride at outsmarting him dissolves as I snuggle up close. The 'game' of hiding would be so calamitous if I were not found.

When I get older, it's as if the roles are reversed. Days, maybe months or even years pass with me feeling that whoever God is, he has gone far away and hidden. My heart aches and I'm not sure why. I wander distracted, strangely lost, and incomplete. Then, in the stillness, I hear his unmistakable voice. Something quickens in my spirit, an urge to reconnect with my maker, but I have lost my bearings and don't know where to look. The voice comes again from a hidden place: *When you search for me, you will find me; if you seek me with all your heart, I will let you find me.* [1] An ancient promise to his chosen people, that their search for God is less a matter of seeking him out in some far-off place and more a case of admitting their wanderlust, their moral failings, and realising that he is beside them all along. Waiting to be found. I want to be included in that promise. The emphasis is less on my efforts in searching and more on the generous self-disclosure of the invisible one being sought.

They can be annoying, careless, untidy, rebellious, loud, and embarrassing. They can interrupt at the wrong moment, they can ask awkward questions, they can wreck our plans, and keep us awake when we are desperate for sleep. But where would we be without children? They are needy yet amazingly resilient, they lack knowledge but are so knowing, they are uncluttered by adult confusions, unbound by adult inhibitions, and unsullied by grown-up deceptions. The highlight of our summers in France is the gathering of our family, four daughters, and their children: the games we play and the better ones the little ones invent, the 'shows' we plan, and the spontaneous spin-offs that emerge. If there were a crowd assembling

---

1   Jeremiah 29:13

in the kingdom, I think we might be surprised at those leading the throng. *Let the little children come to me,* Jesus says, *and do not hinder them; for to such belongs the kingdom of God.'* (Luke 18:16). When it comes to decoding the kingdom, we need look no further.

* * *

Returning to those six, intriguing words – *I will let you find me* – in some ways they encapsulate our two decades in Provence. The stumbling pursuit of a dream, the series of escapades, the pain of mistakes and misunderstandings, the gradual dawning of what kingdom means. We could have bought the flat in north London and, for a season, this would have eased the commute to the city for our dancer daughter. Nothing wrong with that, other than traffic getting heavier and congestion charges getting higher. We could have saved ourselves the demands of learning a new language at a time in our aging lives when even English words seem to regularly go missing. I could have avoided much personal embarrassment at local shops. We could have averted navigating new fiscal regimes – at the last count we were subject to six separate taxes. And if we thought that was bad, Brexit upped the paperwork for Brits with homes in France and pets in tow.

But a kingdom worth following involves searching and seeking with all our hearts. Reckoning ourselves to be so fortunate to have the option, we decided to pursue the idea of a place for the family to gather in the summer. Not a difficult choice perhaps, but it entailed pushing beyond our comfort zones and trying out new customs. What emerged was a slower, more appreciative way of life.

It has not been a venture for the faint-hearted. Starting with an untrustworthy vendor, then brushes with irascible neighbours, blank-faced shopkeepers, an overflowing *fosse*, intermittent wi-fi, 'false friends', border deportations, building site setbacks, tennis ignominy ...none of this was in the plan. But sometimes naivety in a foreign land pays off. We'd have it no other way. Because, as amateurs surfing French waves, we have savoured unlikely dishes, tasted exquisite wines (some that we helped to harvest), made culture-crossing friendships, built up a rich album of memories with our children and grandchildren, and played with an extended palette of watercolours. In short and true to his word, amidst the heady fields of lavender and sun-drenched vines, his kingdom has been revealed in greater depth.... and he has let us find him.

AFTERWORD

If I were to tell you that there is a place that few people know about, that is approached in quiet anticipation, that is entered for free, and where your heartfelt longings will be filled to overflowing, I am guessing you'd be curious?

If I informed you that this place will demand everything you have, you are to bring nothing with you, and there is no turning back once the journey has started, might you have second thoughts?

If I were to say that the place is full of mysteries, unseen stirrings, and scary unknowns yet being there brings strange clarity, divine closeness, and pulsating adventure, would you once again be intrigued?

If I were to add that this place is not far away but right here for those content to be children again, a place that feels like home, and where the curtain between earth and heaven is silk thin, would you be tempted to draw near... even to step in?